THE APPRENTICES

Peter Terson was born in Newcastle-upon-Tyne in 1932. His father was a joiner and he grew up in a world of empty shipyards, dole queues and 'the struggle to bring up the bairns'. He left grammar school when he was fifteen and went into a drawing office, attending with mounting incomprehension at the local technical college till the 'cribbed' formulas on the back of his slide rule were no longer enough to save him and he sank in the face of calculus in his third year.

After two years in the R.A.F., where he trained to be a ground wireless mechanic and washed dishes from Chicksands to Carlisle, he was demobbed in 1952. He decided to be a teacher and after training at Bristol Training College he taught games for ten years without ever mastering the rules of basketball. He wrote plays until, he says, he had enough rejection slips to paper the wall. Eventually he sent a play to Peter Cheeseman at the Victoria Theatre, Stoke-on-Trent, and it was Cheeseman who produced Peter Terson's first play, *A Night to Make the Angels Weep*, in 1965. Then followed *The Mighty Reservoy*, and in 1966 he received an Arts Council grant to be a Resident Playwright at Stoke. At this time Cheeseman 'taught him how to write plays', as he said, and they developed a working partnership, with Terson writing loose scripts and Cheeseman working with him to produce a play which could be altered and varied during rehearsals. This method of work was taken to the extreme in *Zigger Zagger*, for which scenes were written a few days before the first night. In 1967 he left Stoke to go to Whitby in Yorkshire on a hunch that he could write a trilogy for B.B.C. television; this has just been delivered.

Peter Terson has written several plays for television, and his other stage plays are *All Honour Mr Todd*, *I'm in Charge of These Ruins*, *The Rat Run*, *Cadmium Firty*, *The Ballad of the Artificial Mash*, *Jock-on-the-Go*, *Zigger Zagger*, *Mooney and his Caravans*, and an adaptation of *Clayhanger* written with Joyce Cheeseman. In 1967 he shared the John Whiting award with Peter Nicholls; his award being for *Zigger Zagger* and *The Ballad of the Artificial Mash*.

PETER TERSON

THE APPRENTICES

with an introductory note by
MICHAEL CROFT

PENGUIN BOOKS

Penguin Books Ltd, Harmondsworth, Middlesex, England
Penguin Books Inc., 3300 Clipper Mill Road, Baltimore, Md 21211, U.S.A.
Penguin Books Australia Ltd, Ringwood, Victoria, Australia

—

First published 1970
Copyright © Peter Terson, 1970
Introductory material copyright © Michael Croft, 1970
All rights whatsoever in this play are strictly reserved and application
for performance should be made to the author's agents, Margaret
Ramsay Ltd, 14a Goodwin's Court, St Martin's Lane, London WC2

—

Made and printed in Great Britain by
C. Nicholls & Company Ltd
Set in Monotype Baskerville

For
Michael Croft and Peter Cheeseman
two bullies of genius

THE APPRENTICES

The Apprentices was specially written for the National Youth Theatre, which is an organization devoted to the encouragement of drama amongst young people. Its members, who are aged between fifteen and twenty-one and are at school, college or in full-time employment, stage their own productions during the school holidays. The perform annually in the West End of London and have staged many productions in the provinces. They have also undertaken several successful foreign tours and have represented Great Britain at the Festivals of Paris and Berlin. The National Youth Theatre productions of both *The Apprentices* and *Zigger Zagger* have been televised by the B.B.C. as Wednesday Plays.

In his introduction Michael Croft, Director of the National Youth Theatre, describes how *The Apprentices* came to be written and the way in which it developed during rehearsals.

The text of *The Apprentices* has been prepared for publication by Derek Seaton.

A Note on The Apprentices

MICHAEL CROFT

AFTER *Zigger Zagger* it was tacitly agreed that Terson would write another play for the N.Y.T.'s 1968 summer season. Early that year he sent me the first draft of a play called *Prisoners of War*. Unlike *Zigger Zagger* it was fully written, but much as I liked it I did not believe the N.Y.T. could do justice to it, for it needed actors in their mid and late twenties – an age group much more difficult for our young actors to simulate than even middle or old age. Painfully aware that I might be looking a gift-horse in the mouth and, worse perhaps, alienating this marvellous writer from the N.Y.T. for ever, I felt bound to turn the play down.

There the matter rested, and I cast around for another contemporary play. I had still not decided on one when, a few months later, Terson looked in at the rehearsals of *Little Malcolm* which I was then preparing for the Holland Festival. One of the actors was Barrie Rutter, twenty-year-old son of a fish-docker from Hull, who had been in the N.Y.T. for five years. Tough, uncompromising, loyal, warm-hearted and cussed in the true Yorkshire manner, he is a highly-charged natural actor. (Irving Wardle was later to describe him in *The Times* as 'one of the most physically electrifying actors to have appeared since Albert Finney'.) Terson was at once fascinated by him. As he left me that day he asked if I could give him a little more time to try out a new idea based upon 'a character like Rutter'. 'If only I can write it,' he said, 'it could be a beauty.'

Three weeks later when I went up to Whitby where he was working on a lifeboat saga for the B.B.C., I began to share his feeling. He had only written twelve pages (which were sellotaped together along the wall of his study), but the dialogue fizzed and crackled from the page and made me impatient to get to grips with the whole play. 'Could this be It?' asked Terson apprehensively. 'Dare I carry on with it?' I was too exhilarated by what I had read to realize that he thought there might be any doubts about it.

We had started rehearsals of *Zigger Zagger* with only a fragmentary script and a basic idea about the staging. The rest had to be worked out in daily rehearsal. By contrast, we started *The Apprentices* with a fully written play in a fixed setting with a clear line of development. Most writers would have considered that as the main job completed, but to Terson it was still merely a basis for development and he stayed with the company throughout the four weeks of rehearsal, re-writing extensively.

Terson wrote later:

> I drew my characters from different periods of my life and bundled them together in that factory yard. Spow and Garret I knew as boys; Fulcher was a boy I taught in Newcastle a dozen years later; Bagley I know now; Wags got his offer from a talent scout when I was a boy, and so on. I don't want to deter the critics from thinking that the play is about young men in a social dilemma and all that stuff, but for me, it's a lot of people I know, in a place I know, talking about it.

The original version was far more bitter in tone than the one which finally took shape. Bagley was always a major character, a tragi-comic proletarian hero, a marvellous dramatic creation, but at first his decline and failure was obscured because all the other apprentices failed too. Wags, the lovable footballer, failed to get away to Manchester United, the industrious Jeff failed to get promotion and, apart from the brittle-boned Fulcher, who in any case had to come back to a semi-skilled job, the other apprentices showed little interest in either getting away or trying to better themselves. At the same time Bagley himself so dominated the yard that his mates tended to lack colour beside him. Most colourless of all was Red Fred, a stereotyped agitator whom Terson came to dislike so much – 'I can do nothing with this bloody Fred at all!' – that he soon eliminated him entirely. Some of the other characters were equally one-dimensional, like Spow and Garret, who were merely embittered 'old soldiers' taking a vicious delight in the initiation of the new recruits. Terson saw the danger of their becoming caricatures and constantly re-wrote the parts, making them more plausible and more sympathetic.

The first two weeks were spent almost entirely in reading and re-reading the continually changing script, with the actors huddled together over the only available copy and Terson sitting with his head cocked to one side, pencil in ear, mouth slightly agape, eyes half-closed, his characteristic rehearsal posture, like a conductor listening for false notes. He would never interfere during rehearsals, but afterwards we would talk at length over possible cuts and changes. Then he would go back to work in my flat and when I returned late at night I would find him either bashing out new scenes on the typewriter, or kneeling on the carpet with the script spread out in front of him and scissors and sellotape at hand, cutting out unwanted dialogue and sticking in the latest revisions. There were some nights, too, when he had simply given up a scene and gone out in despair.

After two weeks the time sequence had been cut from five years to eighteen months, and the first half was more or less settled. Despite the lack of narrative or psychological development, we felt that it was strong enough dramatically to hold the interest.

The second half was a bigger problem. The danger was that it could easily seem no more than a repetition of the first, in the sense that every scene was set in the same place at the same time of day and in circumstances which limited the development of both action and character. We now began to worry about the outcome with the result that Terson wrote more and more until the second half was twice as long as the first. Finally it reached the playing time of nearly two hours, which I cut by nearly a half at one memorable rehearsal with Terson sitting silent but unflinching beside me, too shocked to point out that I had swept away two vital narrative points and several others essential to their immediate context.

*

Two of the cast allotted to *The Apprentices* had been in the N.Y.T. for several years but there were no obvious parts for them. Terson, who had developed a special relationship with the company, was as much concerned with this as I was, and readily agreed to write them into the play. Thus, while we lost Red Fred, we gained Taffy Doorman and Ramrod the Storekeeper. I believe that these additions gave the play an extra humour and richness. One of the additions, however (Taffy's absurd Richard Burton tale), is patently inadequate, and I must confess that this was not written by Terson at all, but crept into the play at my suggestion. It was based on an endearing story I had heard years before about Burton's father going to see Richard play Henry V at Stratford. Once we started to play about with this tale it got completely out of hand, but rather than spoil the fun, Terson agreed to keep it in.

On the same company basis, a third character, Leo the coloured apprentice, was added for the benefit of a boy who had played the coloured bus conductor in *Zigger Zagger*. But here Terson's intuition failed him. The advent of Leo brought in the colour issue; this had no part in Terson's original conception, and he felt strongly that it was outside the real scope of the play. His solution was to make the apprentices robustly unprejudiced about colour, but in the process poor Leo remained, as Terson readily admitted, as much a stereotype as the frustrated Youth Leader in *Zigger Zagger*.

*

The play moved and excited me from the start but I thought that it was going to be exceptionally difficult to direct. At first I was not certain how we would overcome the lack of plot and repetitiveness of scene and I could not see how I

was going to sort out the various relationships of the apprentices or even make the dialogue audible above the noisy
life of the yard with its continual bursts of football and all
its restless rough-and-tumble.

I cannot direct actors by numbers or work out compli-
cated crowd movements on a stage plan overnight and,
even if I could, I doubt if it would have helped in this case.
I could only play it by ear and ask the actors to do the same.
However, most of the cast had worked together in *Zigger
Zagger* the year before and they reacted wonderfully to
each other from the start. They showed a collective
response and awareness to a degree I had never seen in
twenty years of working with young companies. I ceased
to worry about the outcome and gave the actors their head,
only beginning to force the pace and fix the movement when
a convincing pattern had emerged.

Terson himself revelled in the rehearsals, as he did in the
improvised football games that went on between them (at
times there was little to separate the talk and action onstage
from what was happening off). I had only one fear about the
whole thing. *Zigger Zagger* had had such an outstanding
critical success that I did not believe it could be repeated
so soon afterwards. Having spent their superlatives on one
Terson play, the critics might take a tough line with the
second, and I warned the company accordingly. In any
case, the advance bookings were almost as bad as *Zigger's*
had been – hardly £50 at the box office. But my fears were
unfounded. The critics were almost unanimously enthusias-
tic, and many of them rated *The Apprentices*, as I do, as
being Terson's best play to date.

Indeed I regard it as one of the most significant plays of
our time, not least because it puts the young working people
of this country on the English stage without patronizing
them, vulgarizing them, getting sentimental over them, or
preaching to them, at them, or about them. In the process, I
believe, it shows them to be a great deal more vital
and infinitely more likeable than the more sophisticated
middle-class characters with whom the contemporary

English theatre, for all its experiments, 'happenings', and occasional appearances to the contrary, is still primarily and so boringly concerned.

The Apprentices was specially commissioned by the National Youth Theatre and received its first performance at the Jeannetta Cochrane Theatre, London, in August 1968.

It had the following cast:

DOUGLAS BAGLEY, an apprentice welder	Barrie Rutter
HARRY, an apprentice fitter	Anthony Phipps
'WAGS', an apprentice fitter	Allan Swift
DICKER, an apprentice fitter	Hugh Coldwell
JEFF, an apprentice fitter	John Moran
FULCHER, an apprentice turner	Robert Eaton
BOSWELL, an apprentice fitter	Russell Dixon
JIMMY PASSMORE, an apprentice sheet metal worker	Edwin Shirley
BETTY, a machine minder	Kathleen Lee
LINDA, a machine minder	Paula Wilcox
MABEL, a sheet metal cutting machine operator	Jennifer Galloway
ALICIA, a typist	Maureen Schwarz
LEO, a graduate apprentice	Loftus Burton
SPOW, a fitter and turner	Charles Douthwaite
GARRET, a fitter and turner	John Porzucek
MR BRADBURY, a foreman	Mark Irvine
'RAMROD', a storekeeper	James Gibson
'TAFFY DOORMAN', a doorkeeper	Gareth Thomas
NEW APPRENTICE	Peter Turner

Other Apprentices and Factory Workers:
Stephen Amiel, Stephen Boxer, Martin Chamberlain, Harry Chambers, Thomas Dmochowski, Michael Ford, Alan Hart, Martyn John, Raymond Kemp, Christopher Lacey, Fergus Logan, Brian Payne, Christopher Purnell, Michael Ross, Robert Thompson, Russell Thorpe, Paul Wayne, Albert Welling, Brian Wheeler.
Amanda Allsop, Vivienne Lafferty, Tana Tobin.

Directed by Michael Croft
Assisted by Derek Seaton
Designed by Christopher Lawrence
Lighting by Chris Smith

The play is set in the factory yard of a heavy engineering works in the North of England. The action takes place at 'dinner time' over a period of eighteen months.

ACT ONE

SCENE ONE

The Yard

[*Factory apprentices amble on. Run on. Kicking a ball.*]

WAGS: Make a goal. Clear the pitch. You're in, Dicker.

DICKER: It's always me in.

WAGS: Get in, get in, how's that for a shot?

[*Enter two men with thermos flasks.*]

SPOW: Stop that bloody ball banging about. Stop it, will you?

GARRET: If it knocks over this thermos there'll be trouble.

WAGS: Leave off.

SPOW: Stop that bloody ball banging about. Do I have to get up on my feet to you?

DICKER: Get stuffed.

GARRET: This is a New World thermos, two-pint size.

DICKER: You'll have bladder trouble.

SPOW: You think you're past trouble. It'll come.

DICKER: Go and blow your nose. You're dribbling all over your sandwich.

GARRET: You what? You what?

WAGS: Leave off. We'll do a bit of heading while they have their pap.

SPOW: Pap. I'll pap you, you cheeky bloody thing.

[*Enter girls.* BETTY, LINDA. JEFF *walks by reading a book.*]

BETTY: Watch your head.

JEFF: Sorry.

BETTY: Nearly bumped into you. Just about knocked your print. Is it a good book, luv? Is it sexy?

JEFF: It's a text book, not a sex book.

BETTY: 'Bout work?

JEFF: Aye.

BETTY: Don't you ever want to escape work?

JEFF: I'll escape better when I've mastered it.

BETTY: Oh my my my. Top apprentice of the year.
[She walks on with LINDA.] Do you fancy him?

LINDA: No. He's too quiet.

BETTY: You're not so rowdy yourself.

LINDA: I don't fancy him.

BETTY: I think he fancies you a bit. He's got Linda chalked up on his machine. Hi, not that machine. You look super in hairpins.

LINDA: Do I? Let's put the transistor on and get Bob Miller and his Millermen.

BETTY: Oh, that wonderful band. What would I do without my midday music. Da dah da dum, and it's ... *Parade of the Pops*. I love that feller that sings like Louis Armstrong.

LINDA: He can sing like them all. He's got to sing like them all. It's his job.

BETTY, Why's that then?

LINDA: So he sounds like the groups. He's got to sound like the groups. Do you not get it? Its no use him singing a Louis Armstrong number if he doesn't sound like the groups. Put it on.
[*They hang about jiving in silence, just moving their bodies. Enter* MR BRADBURY.]

MR BRADBURY: Keep that ball down then. It'll be over the wall.

WAGS: He said it'll be over the wall.

DICKER: Can he not think of nothing else but over the wall?

WAGS: Over the wall is his little golden rule in life. It won't go over the wall, Mr Bradbury.

MR BRADBURY: You never know, do you. It might just.

WAGS: But I do know, Mr Bradbury. I know where a ball is going to when I kick it.

MR BRADBURY: You're not a professional yet.

DICKER: When he is he'll send you a ticket, Mr Bradbury. Complimentary.

MR BRADBURY: Are you being funny?

DICKER: No. Complimentary.

[*Enter* DAFT JIMMY *to* JEFF.]

JIMMY: Are you reading, Jeff?

JEFF: Aye, Jimmy.

JIMMY: I won't interrupt you then.

JEFF: O.K. then.

JIMMY: What is it?

JEFF: Diploma stuff, Jimmy. You know.

JIMMY: Is it advanced?

JEFF: C.2.

JIMMY: Shall I tell you what?

JEFF: What's that then, Jimmy?

JIMMY: I started City and Guilds but I failed the course again.

JEFF: That's tough, Jimmy.

JIMMY: C.2 must be a lot harder than City and Guilds, Jeff.

JEFF: Oh, it's hard, but it's easy when you master it.

JIMMY: Can a sheet metal worker get into the drawing office, Jeff?

JEFF: There's vacancies for all trades there.

JIMMY: I sometimes think I won't do it, but I told my mother I would stick in.

JEFF: You do that then, Jimmy.

JIMMY: Did you?

JEFF: What?

JIMMY: Tell your mother you'd stick in?

JEFF: I told my father.

JIMMY: I've got no father.

JEFF: Stick in, Jimmy.

JIMMY: It's the drawing. The technical drawing.

JEFF: I used to enjoy the drawing. The technical drawing. I enjoyed it, the elementary drawing. There's nothing hard about the elementary drawing.

JIMMY: My hands shake.

JEFF: Hah.

JIMMY: And they get sweaty, and it spoils the drawing. If you get sweat under your tee square.

JEFF: That would spoil the drawing.

JIMMY: That's my fault then.

JEFF: It must be, Jimmy.

JIMMY: I'll leave you then.

JEFF: O.K., Jimmy.

JIMMY: If you want me to.

JEFF: All right, Jimmy.

[*Enter* MABEL.]

BETTY: Look at Mabel. What a shame. It is a shame, isn't it? What a rotten shame.

LINDA: And she can't help it. You can't tell her, can you?

BETTY: You know these television advertisements? B.O. Can you tell your best friend. You couldn't start with Mabel, could you? I mean her B.O. isn't as bad as the other stuff.

LINDA: It is a shame.

BETTY: That skin of hers. All the Lifebuoy in the world couldn't wash it smooth.

LINDA: It's the sleep in her eyes gets me. I hate that crust.

BETTY: What a rotten shame. Because she's a nice girl. Under it all. Quite a nice girl, under it all. Look at them legs. If she has babies, them legs will go terrible. I know. I've heard the varicose story off my mother.

LINDA: What a shame.

BETTY: It is a pity.

LINDA: Should we have her over to listen to the Millermen?

BETTY: Let's not, she'll just spoil it.

LINDA: Yes, another time, eh?

SPOW: Watch that bloody ball, my rotten tea near got kicked over.

GARRET: That's a New World thermos, that. And you can't get replacements. Replacements is hard to come by.

[*Enter* MR BRADBURY.]

MR BRADBURY: If that ball goes over the wall there'll be trouble.

SPOW: That's just what we've told them, Mr Bradbury.

GARRET: The general public is over the other side of that. Babies in prams.

SPOW: Old women and old men.

GARRET: I don't care for myself. Except for my thermos. But it's the public I'm thinking of.

MR BRADBURY: I suggested to Mr Raines that there should be a wire netting fence up the top, but no, he said it would lead to a strike. Balls is dangerous.

SPOW: Balls is dangerous, Mr Bradbury. When you're having your lunch.

GARRET: Kicking over your thermos. And your sandwich foil.

WAGS: You can move.

GARRET: We cannot move, why should we move for you young whippersnappers? You can't make us move. Who said we should move. *You move,* move your bloody goalposts.

DICKER: Them goalposts are painted on that wall.

MR BRADBURY: Well, keep that ball low!

[*Enter* BAGLEY *at a run.*]

BAGLEY: Aye, aye, aye.

MR BRADBURY: Bagley!

BAGLEY: Aye, aye aye, here Wags, he's on the ball, look at that control, look at the body swerve, and he's there. Here Wags, Wags, last chance while the goalie's out of position. [*He bangs it over the wall.*] Skied it.

MR BRADBURY: You've put it over the wall, Bagley.

BAGLEY: Have I, Mr Bradbury? Don't worry, Mr Bradbury. You lose too much sleep over that wall, Mr Bradbury.

MR BRADBURY: It's the general public, Bagley, babies in prams.

SPOW: And old women.

BAGLEY: Don't fret, Mr Bradbury. The ball will be returned. There'll be nobody killed out there. No plain clothes constable. It's not going to be brought up at the board meeting. Don't worry yourself, Mr Bradbury. Don't be put out.

MR BRADBURY: It's my responsibility, that wall is. I'm on Wall Patrol.

BAGLEY: Don't worry yourself, Mr Bradbury. You see. Leave it to Bagley. We'll get it back. There'll have been no harm done.

GARRET: It might have landed in the middle of traffic and caused an uproar. And crashes.

BAGLEY: I'll get your ball. Dicker, give me a shoulder.

MR BRADBURY: You're not going over that wall, Bagley.

[BAGLEY *is up on the wall.*]

BAGLEY: Missis. Throw the ball back. Thanks, love. The prisoners are having their recreation hour. Try again, love. Put more body into it. Whee. Try again, love.

MR BRADBURY: Bagley, get down from that wall. The firm has its good name to think about. When you're on that wall you represent the firm.

BAGLEY: Come on, love. Last throw. Here it comes, lads. The prisoners send their thanks to the outside world, love.

[*Ball comes. Big cheer.*]

BAGLEY *to* MR BRADBURY: There's the ball, Mr Bradbury. See, good as new. You worry too much.

MR BRADBURY: You'll be reported for this, Bagley.

BAGLEY: I'll be terribly despondent if you report me, Mr Bradbury. I'd hate my work sheet to get a bad conduct tick on it. If you report me, Mr Bradbury, it means I won't be apprentice of the year this year.

MR BRADBURY: You'll never be apprentice of the year.

BAGLEY: I'd like to be, Mr Bradbury. You have no idea what little burning ambitions there are in this chest. Feel that overall, see, the oil is melting with my burning ambition, Mr Bradbury.

MR BRADBURY: You'll be reported.

BAGLEY: Spoilsport, Mr Bradbury.

[MR BRADBURY *goes.*]

SPOW: Don't be so bloody cheeky, Bagley.

BAGLEY [*to* SPOW *and* GARRET]: The public's outside, Mr Bradbury. Mothers with prams, Mr Bradbury.

SPOW: So there is, you kicking balls over.

BAGLEY: Mothers with babies, Mr Bradbury. Milk feeding,

Mr Bradbury, you never know what'll curdle in this weather, Mr Bradbury.

GARRET: You fellers have it all your own bloody way, don't you?

BAGLEY: A bit of the bad old days is what I want, Garret. A bit of the Army.

GARRET: They'd soon straighten you out.

BAGLEY [*straightening himself out*]: Look at that then, feller, look at that. What did the army do for you?

SPOW: Made a man of him, that's what.

BAGLEY: Flash you.

GARRET: Vulgar lump.

BAGLEY: Sitting there with your New World thermos. Why don't you dine with the workers, eh? Hi, Taffy Doorman, there's a couple of blokes here won't dine with the workers.

TAFFY DOORMAN: Did you ever hear of how the Prince of Wales dined with the workers up in the Durham coalfields in the thirties?

BAGLEY: Prince of Wales, in the thirties. He wasn't born then.

TAFFY: No, the other one, the one that abdicated.

SPOW: They're all related.

TAFFY: Well, he went up to the Durham coalfields, to see the miners, and they invited him in to try their meat and gravy from the soup kitchen. Well, in he went, while all the envoys, and secretarys and kiss-me-arse men waited outside. And inside, the miner finished his gravy, then wiped his plate with his bread. So the Prince of Wales, always good at the etiquette, he did the same. Then afterwards one of his envoys said, 'How did you like the Durham miners, your Highness?' and he was heard to say, 'Charming fellows, but I do hate the way they mop up their gravy!'

BAGLEY: Well, what the hell did that have to do with what I asked you?

TAFFY: Anyone for cards then, boys? Anyone for cards?

DICKER: There he is again, taking pence off children.

TAFFY: At least we're quiet, respectable. Not like them domino maniacs. Right, school assembled. Show your brass or remove your arse.

[BAGLEY *goes to girls*.]

BAGLEY: Hi, girls, turn it up, turn it up. What is it?

BETTY: Bob Miller and the Millermen. Parade of the Pops.

BAGLEY: And ladies and gentlemen, it's *Parade of the Pops*. *Workers' Playtime*, now that you've got a bloody hour off from your lathe we'll give you a tune while you digest your greasy chips. Give us a dance, Betty.

[*He dances with Betty*.]

BETTY: Sexy, isn't he?

LINDA: Isn't he.

BETTY: Is that the only style you've got?

BAGLEY: Yeah, why?

BETTY: You look as though you've got an anchor tied to your whatsit!

BAGLEY: You factory women are so bloody common. So common. I can't bear to be in your company. I'm off.

BETTY: Who do you think would have you, anyway?

BAGLEY: I'm not having a factory tart. I don't want beer mats on my dining-room table.

[*Enter* HARRY.]

Hi Harry, Harry, over here.

BETTY: You won't feed off a table, you'll feed out of a horse box.

BAGLEY: I don't get it. I just don't get it.

[*Girls go hysterical*.]

BAGLEY: Harry, I just don't get it.

HARRY: What don't you get?

BAGLEY: I think I've just been got at. Those tarts have cracked a filthy joke and it went over my head. But I felt it, boy, I felt it.

HARRY: Where did you feel it if it went over your head?

BAGLEY: It must have gone under my head where I felt it. Right in the gut. That's it. That's it. Gerr, you dirty things, factory tarts, never marry a factory tart, the iron filings have got all over, man. Look at them dancing

24

together. You better stay that way, no bloke will ever break you up. How's it going, Harry, you're late out.

HARRY: There were seconds of semolina and jam.

BAGLEY: I can't face the stuff. You're still late, you can't stuff sem down you for this long.

HARRY: I was reading the notice-board.

BAGLEY: What, all the careers advice? Oh, the world is open to you here, boy. It's all laid on, keep your nose to the grind-stone and they'll grind it off. You can get to engineering courses, week-end courses, night courses – but they ain't got the courses we need a course in.

HARRY: It's not a bad life, Doug.

BAGLEY: You're settling in. You're amiable. [*Chants.*] When we get a new apprentice we introduce him to the trade. . . . You took it well, the initiation, you took it well.

HARRY: You've got to, haven't you? Got to take what happens? Better than school.

BAGLEY: You think so?

HARRY: 'Course it is. Better than school. It's all better than school.

BAGLEY: The things we didn't do at school, Harry. Them gym mistresses, man; them little desks on a hot day, what you can do under them. I could sit and listen to them mistresses and watch their blouse buttons heave with emotion when they talked about the Romans . . . my, my, my, what we missed. If we could go back.

HARRY: There's no going back. Besides, your knees wouldn't get under the desk.

BAGLEY: My knees might make it.

HARRY: There's opportunities here though, Doug. Mr Raines said . . . at the interview, about opportunities, if you took all that was offered, he said, with a bit of classes.

BAGLEY: You want to go to classes? All right. I'll go with you. We'll enrol together. The first-year queue is like the start of a race, but kid, once you're off, it's like the Grand National, most of them fall at the first fence, the others string out and one bastard wins at the end of five years, five years, mark you. Still, I'll sign on with you if it'll make you happy. It's near the Billiard Hall.

HARRY: I'd like to give it a try.

BAGLEY: Right, boy. We'll go together.

[*Enter* RAMROD.]

RAMROD: Anyone for the boxing team?

SPOW: That shuts them up.

GARRET: Silence is golden.

RAMROD: Anyone then, eh? Anyone? Come on, it could be the finest team in the works. You're not going to let the moulders take all the cups, are you?

BAGLEY: They can melt them down and make them into brass monkeys for all we care.

SPOW: That's the thanks you get, Ramrod.

BAGLEY: Ramrod. If I had a nickname like that and it turned out to be my straight left, I'd shoot myself.

RAMROD: Come on, Bagley. Make a mixer out of you. Not much difference between you and Billy Walker.

SPOW: Billy Walker was the golden boy. Bagley can be the rusty boy.

RAMROD: Come on, Bagley. Put your guard up and let's see if my ramrod can get through.

BAGLEY: It would need corrugated iron to keep that lot out.

RAMROD: Nobody joining then, eh? Have I to tell the rest of the works that this shop were a set of cissies? That you didn't have spunk? That you've got no shame or manhood?

ALL: Yes!

RAMROD: Don't know how you stick each other. No joiners, eh?

ALL: No.

RAMROD: Right, then. You've missed your chance.

JIMMY: I'll join the team, Ramrod.

RAMROD: All right then. I can work with any material. A willing spirit is worth the first five rounds.

[*Exit* RAMROD *and* JIMMY.]

BAGLEY: Then after that, even that's knocked out of you.

DICKER: Good old Jimmy, we'll turn up to play the Last Post.

TAFFY: Ramrod, his cups and medals are no more good to him now than the iron filings he sweeps up.

GARRET: He was a champion in the Army.

TAFFY: He was a lance-corporal. They told him he would only get on in the army if he excelled at sport; he ended up a punch drunk lance-jack in the Burmese jungle.

SPOW: Bloody hero and champion, that man.

TAFFY: The only man to carry on his training schedule in the Changi Camp. Wales was the home of boxing. I'll tell you a story, but you won't believe it.

BAGLEY: Come on, lads, another Welsh gem.

TAFFY: They say cast down your pearls before swine, but I'll risk it. When I was down the mines, Tommy Farr was fighting Joe Louis; and every round they would send a pit pony with a truck, and on the truck was written in chalk the result of the round; Farr won that round. Round drawn; Joe Louis hurt; oh, this went on for fourteen rounds, pony comes up, stands dumb, chalk message on the back, Farr still there. Then the fifteenth round . . .

ALL: What happened?

TAFFY: Pony came up, stood, looked at us, and said, 'Farr beaten on points.'

VOICES: Go on. Lies. What a story.

TAFFY: That's nothing. That's not even the story. That sort of thing happened every day in Wales.

HARRY: What was the story then?

TAFFY: We killed the pony with a pick and ate it.

HARRY: Why?

TAFFY: He said he'd bet on Joe Louis.

WAGS: Give us the ball then.

BAGLEY: Take it off us, Wags.
How's this for foot-work, Wags?

WAGS: All right. Keep your arse in.

BAGLEY: Nobby Stiles is on the wing, and he comes in.

SPOW: Watch my flask, you biggun.

BAGLEY: I'll come back to you. Take me, Wags.

[WAGS *tackles him and easily takes the ball off him.*
BAGLEY *hacks him.*]

WAGS: Blast my knee. What you doing?

BAGLEY: I'm Nobby Stiles.

WAGS: I might be injured. I've had a belt on the knee.
Look, those boots. You might put me out, you big clown.

BAGLEY: Who you calling a big clown.

WAGS: You I'm calling a big clown. You with those bloody
big feet.

BAGLEY: Don't call me a big clown or I'll push you.

WAGS: Push all you like, but leave my legs alone.

BAGLEY: Say you're sorry for calling me a big clown.

WAGS: I'm not sorry, you could've put me out of action.

BAGLEY: I'd bang you Wags, but I respect your football.

WAGS: Thanks for that much. We'll get on with the game
then.

[*Enter* JIMMY.]

JIMMY: Fight. Fight. Fight.

BAGLEY [to HARRY]: I mean the lad has a fortune in
them legs, with a bit of luck. I wouldn't put him out of
action. I mean you can't injure a man's assets. What if
somebody was to injure my golden looks, the world would
suffer.

JIMMY: Fight. Fight.

BAGLEY: Listen to Daft Jimmy. Just because he's signed on.
Have you signed on then, Jimmy?

JIMMY: Yes, I have, and I'm going to train.

BAGLEY: We better catch him while we can then, Harry,
take our chance while we've got it.

HARRY: One of these days he'll be the boss of us all. Jimmy,
the tyrant of the yard. Get him then, Doug.

BAGLEY: To you, Harry.

HARRY: No, he's not mine.

BAGLEY: Yeah, he is, he's your parcel.

HARRY: He isn't. I don't take daft parcels.

BAGLEY: Jimmy isn't daft, are you, Jimmy?

JIMMY: No, I'm not. So go on.

BAGLEY: To you then, Harry.

HARRY: And you.

BAGLEY: Do you fancy him? He's nice, isn't he?

HARRY: He's all right with that hair.

BAGLEY: He puts his mother's lard on it every night. If you smell it you can smell the remains of fried egg.

BETTY: Leave him alone, you big stiff.

 [JIMMY *escapes*.]

JIMMY: Haaah.

BAGLEY: He's out of the net. After him.

VOICES: Leave him alone. He's all right. Leave him alone. Stop tormenting him.

 [*They chase round the yard and* JIMMY *runs off*.]

 [*Enter* MR BRADBURY.]

BRADBURY: Bagley! You're in for it now!

BAGLEY (to MR BRADBURY): You've got a nasty white spot on your grey overalls, Mr Bradbury.

MR BRADBURY: Mr Raines wants a word with you.

BAGLEY: Are your overalls a nice clean grey or a dirty white, Mr Bradbury?

MR BRADBURY: Enough of that.

BAGLEY: My mother said that your wife lets her washing-up water get tired, Mr Bradbury. That nasty white spot is the birds, she hangs them too near the seagulls.

MR BRADBURY: Your mother has too much to say for herself, Bagley.

BAGLEY: Keep mothers out of it, Mr Bradbury. Eh, lads?

ALL: Keep mothers out of it, Mr Bradbury. Mothers out of it.

MR BRADBURY: You play ball with me and I'll play ball with you. You keep wives out, and I'll keep mothers out.

SPOW: You shouldn't argue with them, Mr Bradbury. It just encourages them.

BAGLEY: Keep my mother out of it, Mr Bradbury.

MR BRADBURY: Now let's not fall out, you and I, Bagley.

BAGLEY: I'm trying to be friendly, Mr Bradbury.

MR BRADBURY (to HARRY): And you can go, lad.

BAGLEY: He's my shop steward. Aren't you, Harry?

MR BRADBURY: You can go, lad! [*to* HARRY.] Now push

off, son, you're getting into bad company and you've only been here days. And you can go too, the lot of you! Mr Raines wants to see you.

BAGLEY: When?

MR BRADBURY: Now. In private.

BAGLEY: If Mr Raines sees me much more in private I won't need a shop steward, I'll need a lawyer. Tell Mr Raines to wait until Bagley is good and ready.

SPOW: You can't do anything with them, Mr Bradbury.

GARRET: I wouldn't have your job for anything.

MR BRADBURY: Posts of responsibility are impossible nowadays. Impossible.

TAFFY: I've got a post of responsibility. I manage.

BRADBURY: You've got an electric gate to keep your troubles out.

SPOW: I wouldn't have a post of responsibility, I really wouldn't, Mr Bradbury.

GARRET: There's nothing to back you up. You're on your own, you see.

BRADBURY: You've said it, you're on your own, you're on your own; the management doesn't give you full support, the shop stewards fight you every inch of the way, these apprentices have no loyalty except to the football team. You're on your own. You've got nothing behind you.

BAGLEY (*standing indecently behind him*): You have got something behind you, Mr Bradbury. [*He dashes off.*]

MR BRADBURY: Did you notice how I pretended not to notice him?

SPOW: Yes.

MR BRADBURY: That's the way I deal with the Bagleys of the world.

GARRET: You handle them well, Mr Bradbury.

[*The hooter goes. They begin to amble off.*]

WAGS: Last shot, Dicker, last shot. Here, let's have a last shot.

HARRY and BAGLEY: Zigger Zagger Zigger Zagger City. Good old Wags. We want our Wagsy, we want our Wagsy.

BAGLEY: Bags I last one in to clock on. Oh, Mabel, you're lovely. Do you love me, Mabel? I could love you, Mabel. If you'd give me a chance. Mabel, I hear the mirrors in your house won't look back at you. Is that right? Bags I last to clock on. Me and my mate. But even he's not quite last. Get in, mate.

SCENE TWO

Fulcher Fight

[DICKER *and* WAGS *come out from dinner.*]

WAGS: Pass, pass. Get in goal and I'll try a spin shot.

SPOW: You first out again?

DICKER: Yeah.

SPOW: You know what'll happen to you?

DICKER: I know what I hope'll happen.

GARRET: You'll get indigestion, that's what you'll get. All this rushing about, straight after a big meal.

WAGS: I diet.

SPOW: Diet or no bloody diet, you'll get indigestion rushing about after dinner. That's how it got me, with me it was sand.

DICKER: *Sand?*

SPOW: In the bloody desert, son, in the bloody desert, that's how I got my indigestion.

DICKER: Stuff the desert.

GARRET: That's the thanks you get, isn't it? When you think, that's the thanks. Remember them speeches in the desert? You're fighting for the unborn, remember them, well these bloody lazy gits are the unborn. They were then.

SPOW: We fought for the unborn. Remember Churchill's speeches? Fighting on the streets, fighting on the beaches, and all that? For the unborn? If I'd bloody known this was the bloody unborn I wouldn't have bloody fought.

[*Others trickle on with* BAGLEY *and* HARRY.]

SPOW: What was for dinner then, Bagley?

BAGLEY: Beef, Yorkshire pudding, spuds, double helpings, peas.

GARRET: I wouldn't bloody touch it.

BAGLEY: You're too bloody mean. Aren't they, Harry? Two mean men?

HARRY: Yeah, they're like Aladdin, sitting there with their flasks. New flasks for old. New flasks for old.

BAGLEY: They're too tight to buy the meal at the canteen.

SPOW: We are not too tight. Fellers like us know what money's worth.

BAGLEY and HARRY: WE DIDN'T HAVE IT EASY.

SPOW: They're some of the unborn we could have done without.

GARRET: He came in the twilight of his mother's life. Her last glorious sunset. She'd been on Guinness, put a bit of spring in her.

TAFFY: Anyone for cards, boys? Show your brass or remove your arse.

[*Enter* RAMROD.]

RAMROD: Right, where's my team?

JIMMY: I'm here, Ramrod.

RAMROD: Right, come on then. For a session.

WAGS: You shouldn't let him train after dinner, he's had a big meal.

RAMROD: He's doing light training.

DICKER: If the firm wants a boxing team they should have time off to box. Not dinner hours.

WAGS: That's right. It's for the glory of the firm.

RAMROD: When we get near the championships we'll get time off.

BAGLEY: Near the championships? You're not putting Jimmy in for championships? Ramrod, there's no violence involved with Jimmy is there?

RAMROD: Between you and me, son, I put gloves on him like cushions, then I put a head guard on, then his gum shield, and then I let him shadow box. Even then I'm worried. Come on, Jimmy.

BAGLEY: Be careful with the boy. A clout on that head from a shadow might damage him for life.

[*They go.* MABEL *enters.*]

BAGLEY: Mabel!

MABEL: Go away.

HARRY: She spoke.

BAGLEY: You spoke, Mabel. You spoke at last. Does this mean I dare have hope, Mabel? Does it mean that I can go through life with a grain of chance?

HARRY: She loves you, Doug. Beneath that overall there lies a heart beating for you, Douglas Bagley.

BAGLEY: Mabel, there's never been anyone but you for me.

BETTY: Leave her alone, you big stiff.

BAGLEY: Oh, get your ear back to the transistor radio. You look as if you're giving yourselves an ear wash. Look at them, what do they look like? Bob Miller and the Millermen. Turn over and get something classic on like symphonies.

BETTY: What do you know about Bob Miller and the Millermen?

BAGLEY: I don't want to know anything about him. Come on, girls, give us a dance. I'm good at balls and functions.

BETTY: We're dancing together.

BAGLEY: Dance with us, and be normal.

BETTY: We'd rather dance together.

BAGLEY: Come on then, Harry, we'll dance together.

[BAGLEY *and* HARRY *dance round yard.*]

GARRET: Look at them silly sods. When we were in Normandy we used to tune in to Vera Lynn, the *Forces* bloody *Favourites,* trying to keep our morale up, charge in with your bayonets, lads, I'm singing you on; and sometimes we'd find a German radio station and they'd be doing exactly the bloody same.

SPOW: Lili bloody Marlene!

GARRET: It would have been bloody cheaper to let the singers fight it out. And us cheer them on.

BETTY: You look disgusting.

BAGLEY: Oh, but it's lovely. Anyway, who the hell wants to

33

dance with you? You're no good to me. I want class.
Hah, there's my style of girl.

[*Office girl goes past.* ALICIA.]

BAGLEY: Hallo, love. Can I escort you across?

ALICIA: I'll manage, thanks.

BAGLEY: You're in the cage of the wild beasts here.

ALICIA: I'm nearly there, thanks.

BAGLEY: I'll wait for you coming out.

ALICIA: I don't mind.

BAGLEY: Who do you serve?

ALICIA: I know you.

BAGLEY: Who do you serve?

ALICIA: Mr Raines.

BAGLEY: Mr Raines. I've been on his carpet many a time.
Have you?

ALICIA: No.

BAGLEY: You ought to try it, it's lovely.

[ALICIA *goes.*]

Harry. Do you know why Mr Raines had a wet mark on
his shirt?

HARRY: Aw, go away.

BAGLEY: Honest, though, do you know why he had a wet
mark on his shirt?

HARRY: No, why did he have a wet mark on his shirt?

BAGLEY: Because his TY-PIST.

[*Re-enter* JIMMY, *jigging.*]

BAGLEY: Hi, Jimmy. What you caught?

JIMMY: Ramrod told me to train out here.

RAGLEY: Is that your style? Bit old-fashioned isn't it?

JIMMY: Ramrod said it'll come back. The old-fashioned
style.

BAGLEY: I'm waiting for a girl, want to stand by me?
Jimmy, do you want to stand by me?

JIMMY: Go on.

BAGLEY: Honest, we'll stand and talk.

JIMMY: Do you, honest?

BAGLEY: Honest, Jimmy. Come on, leave the wall alone.
It's done nothing to you.

JIMMY: Should I?

BAGLEY: Yeah. Come on, there's a typist coming out. I'll keep her talking and you can touch her leg. Stop jumping about, she doesn't like sweaty boys.

HARRY [*to the girls*]: What's that, then?

BETTY: Bob Miller and the Millermen.

HARRY: He's all right, isn't he? He sounds all right.

BETTY: He's good to dance to.

HARRY: That bit there, you know who that reminds me of? It reminds me of ... what's his name, that pop number, what's it, you know, Jimmy Swift ...

LINDA: He's meant to sound like Jimmy Swift.

HARRY: That's good, that. Sounding like that. Jimmy Swift.

LINDA: They've got a singer there can take off anybody, anybody you care to name, he can take them all off.

HARRY: Yeah. He's good, what's *his* name then?

LINDA: I don't know.

BETTY: Linda's seen it, haven't you Linda?

LINDA: Yes. I've seen it, live.

HARRY: Live?

LINDA: Live. They do it from London, you know.

HARRY: In some sort of hall is it?

LINDA: It's in a small theatre near the river.

HARRY: The Thames?

LINDA: Yes. A small theatre there.

HARRY: Like a studio?

LINDA: That's it. But it's a theatre, seats and that, and gilt, and, you know, gold cherubs and all that on the ceiling, and they have plush seats, and boxes, where the rich used to sit, but now the boxes are ... like, turned into a glass studio.

BETTY: She's actually been in.

HARRY: Where do you get your tickets from?

LINDA: You get them free, if you ask. How it happened to us like, me and a friend, we were walking along the embankment, and there was these paintings, like hung up, with all the artists sitting by them, by the railings.

HARRY: What were the artists like?

35

LINDA: Super, beards and everything; and some of the women, heeh, what a sight.

HARRY: Were they? They really live, don't they?

LINDA: Yes.

HARRY: You don't see anybody hanging paintings up on the park railings in this town.

BETTY: They'd get filthy in five minutes.

LINDA: It was like Paris.

HARRY: You been to Paris as well?

LINDA: I'm going next year if my mum gets fit for the coach.

HARRY: I'd like to see Paris. But I suppose I'll have to see London first.

LINDA: I think it's best.

HARRY: London?

LINDA: To see London first.

HARRY: What about Bob Miller and his Millermen?

LINDA: Well, we had an ice cream, then a coffee, and you know what your feet get like in London, mine were red, and I thought, I've got to get my shoes off, so we went over the road, and there was this queue, and we had nothing else to do, you know what it's like, and we said to this girl, 'What you queuing for?' and she said, 'Bob Miller and the Millermen, live' and we said, 'Where do you get your tickets?' and she said, 'In there.' So we went, got tickets, stood back in the queue, and got in.

HARRY: Was it super?

LINDA: Super. Best thing we saw in London.

HARRY: Was Bob Miller super?

LINDA: Super. Live.

HARRY: And do they do their turns? Live?

LINDA: Oh, yes. And they're watching the clock all the time. See how the time's going along. They've got to be dead exact, and there's this performer, he does these voices. Listen.

HARRY: Is that him?

LINDA: Yes.

BETTY: Linda's put a request in for her birthday.

HARRY: Have you?

LINDA: Yes.

HARRY: When is it?

LINDA: Today. I've sent it in for today.

HARRY: Hi. Can I listen?

LINDA: Yes. It's the song by Louis Armstrong that this other one takes off so well.

HARRY: Does he sing his own numbers?

LINDA: No. He's not good enough. He's just good at taking others off.

BETTY: Should we ask Mabel if she wants to listen?

LINDA: Let's.

BETTY: Mabel, love, Mabel. Come on, have a listen, Linda has a request in. Poor thing, she's a bit plain.

LINDA: But we're good to her.

BETTY: Come on, Mabel love.

BAGLEY: Come on, Harry.

BETTY: There's your master. You should learn to bark for him.

HARRY: She's got a request in.

BAGLEY: Request?

HARRY: Yeah.

BETTY: Does he own you? Or are you just on hire like an evening suit?

BAGLEY: Let's get this typist.

HARRY: I'm listening for this request.

BAGLEY: What is it?

HARRY: What is it? The request?

LINDA: 'Green Leaves'.

HARRY: 'Green Leaves'.

BAGLEY: They'd look bloody funny any other colour.

BETTY: They could be brown in autumn, funny trap.

BAGLEY: Get out of it.

LINDA: Or red, tell him.

BETTY: Or red.

BAGLEY: Come on, Harry, let's get this typist.

HARRY: I'm listening for the request.

BAGLEY: Is it your Golden Wedding Anniversary or something?

BETTY: Why don't you lead your own life?

HARRY: I *do* lead my own life.

BETTY: I'd say he leads the life for both of you.

BAGLEY: Come on, Harry, let's get a decent girl.

HARRY: It's all right. They might play it.

BAGLEY: They might play it! My mother once requested Sandy McPherson and his Organ Down in the Glen. She never got over the shock of his selections.

[*Re-enter* ALICIA.]

BAGLEY: Say hello, Jimmy.

JIMMY: Hello.

ALICIA: Let me by then.

JIMMY: Hello, then.

ALICIA: Hello, now let me by.

JIMMY: Aw.

BAGLEY: You'll have to let her by, Jimmy, she's said hello.

JIMMY: All right then. Pass unmolested.

BAGLEY: He reads American comics. Can I see you over the yard, Alice?

ALICIA: Had your spies out?

BAGLEY: Oh, I keep my car to the typewriter keys. Look at them, with their ears to that. They've got a request in to Bob Miller and the Millermen. Do you make requests?

ALICIA: I don't go in for that sort of thing.

BAGLEY: You go in for quiet drinks and a dance, don't you? I've seen you at the Plush Four nibbling cheeselets and some sucker's sherry before the dance.

ALICIA: I haven't seen you.

BAGLEY: Under this greasy uniform is a lad who could make you comfortable. Say when, then.

ALICIA: I don't mind. If you like. We'll fix a night.

BAGLEY: All right then. I'm free every night except Saturday and Sunday.

ALICIA: Saturday and Sunday?

BAGLEY: Saturday we go wild after the football match, and

Sunday is too solemn for anything. But any other night. At your convenience.

ALICIA: At your convenience.

[*She goes.* BAGLEY *to girls.*]

BAGLEY: You thought I wouldn't. You were watching out the corner of your Bob Millermen eyes.

BETTY: We weren't watching. We didn't notice, we don't care.

BAGLEY: You were watching. Ha, ha, make mine office style.

BETTY: He thinks he's seen the world. But he's just a backyard tom cat.

[*Enter* FULCHER.]

FULCHER: They're all the same, Bagley. They're all the same.

BAGLEY: Yes. To you, Fulch, to you they're all the same.

FULCHER: They're all the same, Bagley, all the same.

BAGLEY: They're all the same to *you*. You have no imagination. To you, the feminine gender of anything is to buck; but there are distinctions, fine distinctions if you have any finesse. You have nothing. You've got no more subtlety than the north pole of a magnet going to the south. Isn't that right, Jeff?

JEFF: What's that, Doug?

BAGLEY: What's the rule of bar magnets?

JEFF: Unlike poles attract, like poles repel.

FULCHER: You shut up and keep out of it. You keep your nose in that book. Get back to night schools, or I'll shut your nose in that book and snip it off.

BAGLEY: Fulcher. Your argument is with *me*. Don't think you're tough because you've been in Borstal. I know what you lot are in there, set of bedwetters, set of urinetics, set of bloody social science cases.

FULCHER: You said what?

BAGLEY: I said it's my fight.

JIMMY: Fight, fight.

BETTY: We're trying to get Bob Miller and his Millermen.

SPOW: Watch that bloody thermos. You can't get refills.

JIMMY: Fight, fight, big fight.

BAGLEY: Come on then, Fulcher.

FULCHER: Right, you picked it, you have first hit.

BAGLEY: No, just get stuck in, just get stuck in.

FULCHER: Go on, start it, I dare you, start it, go on, and by God you'll be sorry.

BAGLEY [*pushing*]: I've started it. Try that.

FULCHER: That's not starting it. I mean, get me roused. If you can. Rouse me with a blow and by God, you'll be sorry.

BAGLEY: Try that then, get roused.

FULCHER: You're trying to rouse me, aren't you?

BAGLEY: Sure.

FULCHER: Well, you're not succeeding. But if you do, I'm warning you, you'll be sorry.

[*Enter* MR BRADBURY.]

MR BRADBURY: What's this? Fighting? Stop this fighting. Fighting. Like a lot of bloody kids.

GARRET: It's no wonder there's such violence in the world, Mr Bradbury.

MR BRADBURY: Now break it up, or you'll be in front of Mr Raines, the pair of you.

BAGLEY: I wouldn't go *anywhere* in his company.

MR BRADBURY: You'll go in front of Mr Raines with him if I report you.

BAGLEY: Not with that runny nosed snot, I wouldn't.

JIMMY: Lemme at him, lemme at him.

FULCHER: You what? You daft bastard. [*Chases* JIMMY *round the yard.* JIMMY *knocks thermos over.*]

[BAGLEY *grabs* FULCHER.]

BAGLEY: Look! Your argument is with me, not with Jimmy, now *scram*.

FULCHER: One of these days I'll get you, Bagley, and don't you bloody forget it! [*He goes.*]

GARRET: Oh, my New World. It's gone. It's gone.

SPOW: Now look what's happened.

GARRET: The finest vacuum made in Britain that.

SPOW: And look at me corned-beef sandwiches.

DICKER: What with corned-beef and tea your bladders must look like a gypsy's arse.

GARRET: He'll have to pay for this, Mr Bradbury. He'll have to pay for this.

BAGLEY: He won't pay for it. He was chased.

SPOW: It'll have to come out of his pay packet.

HARRY: You won't touch pay packets.

APPRENTICE: It was Fulcher's fault, not Jimmy's.

HARRY: You won't touch pay packets.

BAGLEY: I wouldn't pay to keep his bladder filled.

GARRET: It'll have to come out of somewhere, thermos flasks aren't made out of nothing.

MR BRADBURY: Nobody said anything about pay packets.

SPOW: It'll come out of something.

BAGLEY: I'm paying nothing.

GARRET: It was Bagley, he kicked it.

SPOW: And it's seeped through my overalls.

GARRET: It doesn't stop here, you know, it doesn't stop here, I'm taking this further. I won't be satisfied to let it rest.

JEFF: Appeal against your Income Tax for it.

GARRET: And you can bloody shut up for a start!

MR BRADBURY: I'll have to report to Mr Raines.

HARRY: Stuff Mr Raines.

VOICE: After you with Mr Raines.

BETTY: She's got it, they're playing it. Listen, for Linda Fox, listen.

COMPÈRE: ... for you, Linda, and all your friends in the factory yard, by special request, Bob Miller and his Millermen with 'Green Leaves'.

[*They all stand and listen in silence.*]

LINDA: And it's the last request of the day.

[*Hooter goes. They all go in to work.*]

ALICIA [to BAGLEY]: Mr Raines has noticed that you're always a minute behind clocking on. Don't think he missed it.

BAGLEY: So long as you haven't missed him, missing it.

ALICIA: An act of defiance, he calls it. A minor act of petty defiance.

BAGLEY: It makes me feel good though, love. A minor act of petty defiance every day makes me feel good over the years.

SCENE THREE

Initiation

[SPOW *and* GARRET. *Enter new* APPRENTICE.]

SPOW: You a new apprentice then, son?

BOSWELL: Yes. I've just started.

SPOW: Has your Mum ironed your overalls?

GARRET: Funny time of year to start.

BOSWELL: I had tried to stay at school, then left. I'm a special case.

SPOW: We're all bloody special cases here, son. Aren't we, Garret? Special cases.

GARRET: You'll be a special case afore long.

SPOW: You must be a special case to come here. There's lots of openings in the world without locking yourself in behind those prison walls.

BOSWELL: You're in.

SPOW: In our days things were worse.

GARRET: You had to be grateful for what you got.

SPOW: You were glad to get in anywhere.

GARRET: There were queues to be an apprentice in them days.

SPOW: And if you could get on the Railway ...

GARRET: Or police ...

SPOW: Or owt pensionable like that, why you thought you were in luxury.

GARRET: But now, you get it all for nowt.

[*Enter* BAGLEY *and* APPRENTICES.]

BAGLEY: When we get a new apprentice ...

ALL: We introduce him to the trade,

Down with his trousers,
See if he can make the grade.
   [*They initiate him.*]

VOICES: In, grease him up. Harder than that man, let's hear him. Come on, grease his nipple.

BETTY and LINDA: Leave him alone. Leave him be. Can you not see he's had enough, leave him be.

VOICES: Keep bloody out of it. Keep bloody out of it. Once girls were done.

BETTY and LINDA: Leave him be. Leave him be.
   [*They stand back.*]

BETTY: Now look what you've done, he's crying.

LINDA: Let him get up.

BAGLEY: Why, it was nothing.

BETTY: Look what you've done. You big stiff. It's all right for you, you bloody bull, you can take it.

BAGLEY: You can take it, can't you kid?

SPOW: Are you O.K., son? He's got spectacles on.

BAGLEY: Why didn't somebody say he had spectacles on? Are they bust, son?

BOSWELL: No. I thought they were. They're not.

BAGLEY: Are you all right then? Course you are, aren't you, son? All right? You must be all right. You're just crying for your specs, son, aren't you?

BOSWELL: Yes.

BAGLEY: He's just crying about his specs, you see. He thought they were broken. Why, he took it well, didn't you, kid? You've got to take it. He took it.

TAFFY: I don't know what you want to be doing that for. It's bloody dangerous, not to say vulgar.

DICKER: He's a Welsh Puritan.

TAFFY: I'm against it, man. It's like *Tom Brown's Schooldays*.

BAGLEY: It's a tradition. Like Welsh Rarebit.

TAFFY: Traditions in Wales are beautiful. Not vulgar like this.

HARRY: Wales is beautiful. I've been there camping, mountains and lakes.

TAFFY: I don't like your English traditions, your flaming Morris Dancers, and rugby players hanging knickers on goal-posts.

BAGLEY: What about Welsh rugby players and their leeks.

TAFFY: The leek is a more manly symbol than a pair of knickers. And as for this habit, this initiation, I think it's barbaric.

BAGLEY: It isn't barbaric. I had it.

WAGS: What does that prove? I think Taffy is right. Do away with it.

JIMMY: Keep it in. I like it.

TAFFY: There we are, that split personality likes it. You better do away with it.

JEFF: I think it would be best done away with.

BAGLEY: The moulders make a mould of their apprentices, don't they? And the pattern makers nail them to a pattern; we'll have nothing left.

HARRY: It'll hit the tourist industry.

TAFFY: Well, I say do away with it. Just take an apprentice in. Do something symbolic if you like. Like crossing the equator on a ship.

GARRET: We did that on the troopships, that's good fun. With old Father Neptune.

BAGLEY: Old Father Neptune? He would die for want of sea water up here.

HARRY: He could come by canal.

BETTY: I think it should be done away with. Especially with girls around.

SPOW: Girls used to do it worse than the men once upon a time.

GARRET: Do you remember what they used to do in the Rope Works?

JIMMY: What did they do in the Rope Works?

GARRET: Has the boxing knocked your imagination out of you?

SPOW: And the ropes were all gauges.

BETTY: This isn't the Rope Works.

LINDA: And that was before the war.

44

TAFFY: Do away with it. If I can get you to do away with it then my departure from Wales will not have been in vain.

BAGLEY: Look, the kid doesn't mind. Do you, kid?

BOSWELL: No. I don't mind.

JEFF: Now it's over. Nobody minds once it's over. They want to see somebody else receive it.

JIMMY: Don't spoil the sport. Keep it on.

BAGLEY: We'll take a vote on it. I'll make the closing speech. Gentlemen, lads, fellow lads, any others; women-folk; I support the retention of initiation because it makes us all a band of brothers, happy brothers, we few, standing at our machines. Other societies have it, the Freemasons, the Buffaloes, the Order of the Garter –

TAFFY: If you think, to get the Order of the Garter, you get your testicles plastered then you must be mad.

SPOW: It would have ruined Montgomery at his age.

JEFF: I'm with Taffy, I'm against the Initiation. I think it's humiliating. I think it's just kept on to give the *old men* a thrill.

SPOW: Who are you looking at, you cheeky lump.

BETTY: I'm against it. This is a mixed yard.

LINDA: We don't like your nasty habits.

BAGLEY: What does Mabel think?

HARRY: It's her only form of enjoyment.

BETTY: Leave Mabel out of it. That's the trouble with you, Bagley. You always turn on the quiet ones. You don't know what it's like to be hurt. You've got no feelings.

BAGLEY: I've got feelings. I wept buckets when City lost the Cup.

JEFF: Let's have a vote on it then. Who is in favour of the abolition of the Initiation? All in favour say Aye.
    [*Not many.*]

BAGLEY: Now, vote for retention. And never mind this mumbling in your shirt collars. I want to see hands up. See who's voting.

JEFF: That's intimidation.

BAGLEY: It isn't. I just want to know who my friends are. Hands up, if you wish to retain the traditions of the factory, the historical usages of the firm, the long line of continued development of the yard ...

JEFF: If Mr Raines could hear you now, there'd be a rush to the Stock Exchange to buy shares.

BAGLEY: Hands aloft.

[*Hands go up. Enter* MR BRADBURY].

MR BRADBURY: Bagley! what's this? A strike meeting?

BAGLEY: Yes, Mr Bradbury, we're all walking out. Exodus. I'm Moses. We're off to Freedom, Mr Bradbury. Tell Mr Raines, the machines will have to mind themselves.

MR BRADBURY: What is it now, lads? You've got nothing to complain about. We don't want trouble here, this isn't the Motor Works ... you've got a Welfare Officer.

BAGLEY: Stop worrying! Right lads, motion unanimously carried.

[*The crowd disperses.*]

BAGLEY: You all right, son? Sure you're all right, son?

BOSWELL: Yes.

BAGLEY: What's your name then?

BOSWELL: Boswell. Osmund Boswell.

BAGLEY: Bloody hell! A good job we didn't know before or we'd have murdered you. Hi, there! Watch Bagley's twinkling feet.

[JIMMY *and* BOSWELL.]

JIMMY: Have you got a big brother?

BOSWELL: No.

JIMMY: Not called Tommy?

BOSWELL: No, I haven't.

JIMMY: Tommy Boswell?

BOSWELL: I have a sister.

JIMMY: It must have been another name. See him there, him with the ball now, he's got the makings.

BOSWELL: Has he?

JIMMY: Not him with the ball now, the one who had the ball, like, he's got the makings. So they say like. They say he's got the makings. I wouldn't really know. Not really, like I don't follow football the way Dicker does, but they say he's got the makings. He's good on his feet.

BOSWELL: He looks good on his feet.

JIMMY: Football isn't my game.

BOSWELL: Isn't it?

JIMMY: No. Football isn't my game. Not football.

BOSWELL: He looks good.

JIMMY: Guess what is my game.

BOSWELL: What is your game?

JIMMY: Boxing.

BOSWELL: You a boxer then?

JIMMY: Yes. But I'm too early to bring on yet. That's what my trainer says. I'm too early to bring on. He doesn't want to put me in among the heavies yet.

BOSWELL: Why doesn't he put you among the lights?

JIMMY: I'm too heavy for the lights. I carry a lot of weight, but I don't carry the punch of the heavies.

BOSWELL: He looks good on his feet.

JIMMY: I'm good on my feet. The trainer says. For a heavy. I could keep out of the way of trouble, but not yet. Have you got a girl then?

BOSWELL: No, I've just left school. I stayed on.

JIMMY: What school?

BOSWELL: St Hilda's.

JIMMY: You a Catholic then?

BOSWELL: No.

JIMMY: Shake on it, I'm not either. See Bagley, he knocks off Mr Raines' secretary. She comes out and leaves him fags in the yard. She's mad about him.

BOSWELL: Who's Bagley?

JIMMY: You know Bagley.

BOSWELL: Is that him?

JIMMY: Yeah, he says if I go to the dance like, he can fix me up, with a woman. Not a typist I don't suppose, but some woman, but I live out in the country.

BOSWELL: Do you?

JIMMY: Yes. Do you live out?

BOSWELL: No. I live in.

47

JIMMY: Haaah. Look, there's Bagley's girl. Typist.
   [ALICIA *to* BAGLEY.]
BAGLEY: Hello, Alice. I'm glad to see you.
ALICIA: I should hope so.
BAGLEY: Little fracas.
ALICIA: When did that last upset you?
BAGLEY: Well, this one did. Never mind, did you get home
   last night?
ALICIA: Yes. Do you want a cigarette?
BAGLEY: Thanks, love. That's the new lad.
ALICIA: Yes, I know, we did his cards up in the office.
BAGLEY: Osmund Boswell. Ha, I said to him, 'If we'd
   known your name was Boswell, we'd have murdered
   you.'
ALICIA: Yes. Douglas, I think there is a chance of us getting
   away together for the holidays.
BAGLEY: Fooling your parents for a night is bad enough,
   let alone a fortnight.
ALICIA: But up at the club, there was a list up on the board,
   a holiday in Dorset, I just wondered, you know, it's an
   exchange trip to a club down there. If *our* lot should go,
   supposing it doesn't clash with the French trip, then I
   could put my name down, and if you booked in near,
   then when I got down there, providing Laurie isn't
   going, then we could have a fortnight together.
BAGLEY: Who is he?
ALICIA: Who?
BAGLEY: Boswell. Why is he starting now?
ALICIA: Did you hear what I said about the holiday?
BAGLEY: It sounds a bit worrying.
ALICIA: You worry! It's my worry.
BAGLEY: It would be on my mind, it might put me off.
ALICIA: That would be the day.
BAGLEY: Who is the kid? He's late in starting.
ALICIA: Oh, he left school last September, but he had a bit
   of a breakdown.
BAGLEY: Nervous?
ALICIA: Yes.

BAGLEY: Bit early for nervous breakdowns, isn't it?

ALICIA: It's something that runs in the family. His sister had it.

BAGLEY: Nervous breakdowns don't run in the family, do they?

ALICIA: Something does.

BAGLEY: Poor kid.

ALICIA: Are we thinking about it then?

BAGLEY: What?

ALICIA: The summer holidays.

BAGLEY: I think of nothing else.

ALICIA: I better dash. Mr Raines is having an early lunch. Shall I leave you a fag?

BAGLEY: Thanks, love.

ALICIA: Spoilt. [*She goes.*]
  [WAGS *and* DICKER.]

WAGS: I said to my Dad, 'I want to be a professional footballer, Dad,' like I keep prodding him, to keep it in his mind.

DICKER: What did he say?

WAGS: He said I should learn my trade.

DICKER: What did you say?

WAGS: I said, 'Football will be my trade.'

DICKER: So what did he say?

WAGS: He said, 'There aren't any good fighters now,' he said, 'Jack Dempsey was the last of the good fighters, because he was a hungry fighter, you've got to be hungry to be a fighter.'

DICKER: But that's boxing.

WAGS: That's what I said, 'That's boxing,' I said, but he said, 'Same with football, you've got to be hungry to be a good footballer.'

DICKER: So what did you say?

WAGS: I said, 'If I learn my trade, I'll have a job, I won't be hungry.'

DICKER: What did he say to that?

WAGS: He said I wouldn't be hungry anyway because I'd be on National Assistance.

DICKER: He's not very logical, your old man, is he?

WAGS: He works on the brewery wagons, but he's been upset since the breathalyser. They used to drink at every pub, sometimes they'd have eleven pints a day then bring the wagons home, now he can't. It's a brewery rule since the breathalyser.

DICKER: What's that got to do with your football?

WAGS: It's like you said. It's made him all illogical.

[*Enter* FULCHER *with his gang.*]

FULCHER'S GANG:

When we got a new apprentice,

We introduce him to the trade.

FULCHER: Where is he then, where's the kid? Come out, come out, wherever you are. There he is.

BAGLEY: Fulcher. Stop it, he's been done.

FULCHER: Not by us, he hasn't.

BAGLEY: He's been initiated. Now leave off.

FULCHER: Who says like?

BAGLEY: I say like.

FULCHER [*feinting*]: Fetch him, lads.

BAGLEY: Fulcher. If you do him, I'll do you. And all your bloody gang.

[*They face up.*]

FULCHER: One day, Bagley, I'm going to get you.

BAGLEY: Well, I'll be around.

FULCHER: Well, I won't. I won't be around. I've signed up for the bloody army, mate. I'm getting out. And you'll be sorry, when I get back, you'll be sorry. I'm joining the fighting mob, mate, and you'll be bloody sorry.

BAGLEY: Well, I'm trembling like.

FULCHER: You're too heavy for me yet, mate; I don't fight over weight.

BAGLEY: What weight are you?

FULCHER: I'm not telling.

BAGLEY: You're heavier than me, that's why.

FULCHER: I am not.

HARRY: Yes you are. Great bloody lump.

VOICE: What you doing, Fulcher?

HARRY: He's joining the pioneers. He's as thick as a shovel.

VOICE: He's joining the Peace Keeping Force of the United Nations.

DICKER: He's joining the Gorillas. Yugh. Yugh.

BAGLEY: What you joining, then? I thought the women's services were being run down.

HARRY: Run down and worked up if Fulcher gets in.

FULCHER: I'm not joining them.

JIMMY: What you joining then?

FULCHER: Thick pig. I was going to keep it a secret but I won't now. I'm joining the paratroopers.

BAGLEY: Paratroopers. You, dangling on the end of two hundred square feet of artificial silk.

FULCHER: I'm joining the paratroopers. The free fall squad. I'm getting my jumps in.

BAGLEY: You'll break your bloody neck.

JEFF: The strain when a parachute opens is quite a poundage.

FULCHER: I know all that. I've had the tests.

JEFF: You don't drift down, like it looks on the pictures. You come down at a terrific velocity.

FULCHER: I know that. I've had the tests.

HARRY: What speed do you think you come down at?

FULCHER: Feet per second. See that wall? They make you jump off a wall that high, for your suitability test.

BAGLEY: What a liar, you couldn't stand the height, let alone jump it.

FULCHER: Wanna bet, Bagley?

BAGLEY: Dollar.

FULCHER: Right. Jump off that wall? For a dollar?

BAGLEY: Bet's on.

FULCHER: Now I'll call your bluff, Bagley.

BAGLEY: No bluff. Up there.

FULCHER: Right, then. Right, I'll show you. Who'll hold the bets?

MATE: I'll hold them.

BAGLEY: There's my dollar, says he can't jump that bloody wall.

51

FULCHER: Right, who'll lend me a dollar? I left mine in the toilets.

VOICES: Go on. Hoah.

FULCHER: I can get a dollar out of the toilets.

BAGLEY: Is it you that pinches out of the pockets then?

FULCHER: Calling me a thief then?

BAGLEY: I'm calling you every bloody thing, but first things first. I'm saying you can't jump that bloody wall. Paratrooper.

FULCHER: On then. I'm going up. Right. Give us a bunkup.
[*They bunk him up.*]
Is this where you want me? This where you want me to stand?

BAGLEY: Stand anywhere.

FULCHER: This is the height you have to jump to get in the paras. If anything, this is lower. What you do, see, you jump, and tuck. Jump and tuck. You don't keep your legs stiff, you jump and tuck and then forward roll, like . . .

VOICES: Go on then. Get on with it.

FULCHER: I'll change my position. Along here, it'll be better, it's higher. Is this O.K.? Yes. This is about the height. And we jumped onto concrete.

ALL: Get on with it!

FULCHER: Do you want to raise the bet?

BAGLEY: No. Bloody well jump.

FULCHER: Well give me some room then.

ALL: Ten. Nine. Eight . . .

FULCHER: Eh! Clear away that debris!

ALL: Hoah.

BAGLEY: Get on with it. Less the blather. Put a time limit on him.

JEFF: Countdown. Ten, nine . . .

ALL: Eight, seven, six, five, four, three . . .
[*Enter* MR BRADBURY.]

MR BRADBURY: Fulcher, get off that wall.

ALL: Two, one . . .
[FULCHER *jumps. Lands badly. Loud snap.*]

MR BRADBURY: Stand aside. Stand aside. Send for the ambulance man, quick. Somebody send for the ambulance nurse.

SPOW: He's broken something.

GARRET: Full of talk, these kids, full of talk. When I was in the army, Christ, I'd jump over that if the Jerries were behind me.

SPOW: They've got nothing to back them up. They landed us in bloody Germany from parachutes. Two weeks training. That's the bloody training I got. Two weeks.

[*Enter* RAMROD *with stretcher.*]

RAMROD: Let me see him, let me see him. Come on, clear away.

MR BRADBURY: I think it's a break, Ambulance.

RAMROD: All right, all right. We want no guessing. Somebody responsible unroll the stretcher. Jimmy, you. Unroll the stretcher.

JIMMY: Yes, Ramrod.

RAMROD: Now, let me see it.

MR BRADBURY: It seems to be a break, on the ankle.

RAMROD: If a guess was worth anything we'd all be qualified ambulance men, wouldn't we? Let me see. Yes. Stretcher. I'll need the stretcher.

JIMMY: I'm in a tangle. How do you do it?

DICKER: Here, I'll do it. You couldn't get out of the way of a one way street.

RAMROD: Right. Are we ready?

MR BRADBURY: What is it?

RAMROD: I'm afraid it's a break. Ankle.

MR BRADBURY: That's what I said.

RAMROD: I'm not guessing. Right, clear away. Somebody responsible hold the other end. Jimmy.

[*They lift* FULCHER *up and carry him off.*]

FULCHER: That's my dollar, Bagley.

MR BRADBURY: Now break it up, the lot of you. How many times have I told you to keep clear of that wall? It's a dangerous wall, and I've told you and told you umpteen times.

SPOW: You have told them, Mr Bradbury, we've heard you.

MR BRADBURY: Umpteen times, haven't I, umpteen times.

ALL: Umpteen times.

[*Hooter goes.*]

MR BRADBURY: Now get in. Mr Raines will look sick when he sees them time clock sheets. We're losing man hours by the bloody hundred. And you, Bagley, were involved in this.

BAGLEY: There's only one thing, Mr Bradbury. Would you call it a 'jump' or a 'fall'. Do I lose my dollar?

MR BRADBURY: He's broken an ankle. Have you no sympathy?

BAGLEY: None whatsoever.

MR BRADBURY: Then there must be something wrong with you, Bagley.

BAGLEY: I'm thinking, for once, you must be right. I'm last to clock on.

MR BRADBURY: You'll be before Mr Raines, Bagley.

BAGLEY: That man is beginning to smell of after shave lotion.

MR BRADBURY: Well?

BAGLEY: At midday? And it isn't Old Spice either, it's more old lace. Hi, Harry, where did those two say they were going for their holidays?

HARRY: Keep it to yourself. Ilfracombe. Where are we?

BAGLEY: Away, Harry. Away. Like bloody pigeons, boy. Away, out of the net.

HARRY: Eh. Let's go in the paratroopers.

BAGLEY: You what?

[HARRY *limps.*]

Oh, yes! 'I've sprained my ankle.'

HARRY: 'Do you want to raise the bet?'

[*They both limp off.*]

SCENE FOUR

Long Hot Summer

[WAGS *and* DICKER.]

WAGS: I knew he was there, this scout. I knew he was there.

DICKER: How did you know him?

WAGS: I kept my ear to the ground. Funny thing was, he wasn't there to watch me.

DICKER: Go on, who was he there to watch?

WAGS: The opposing centre half.

[*Enter* JIMMY.]

JIMMY: Hear you got spotted, Wags.

WAGS: Yeah, did Jimmy. They were there watching the opposing centre half, really.

JIMMY: But they spotted you?

WAGS: I'll tell you some time, Jimmy.

JIMMY: Right then, mate. That's a date, feller.

[*Enter* SPOW *and* GARRET.]

SPOW: Hear you got spotted, Wags.

WAGS: Don't let it turn your head then, Spow. You old fellers shouldn't get ideas.

SPOW: You got spotted like a dalmatian gets spotted, from its arse to its tip.

GARRET: These young 'uns are always being bloody spotted for something or the other, pop singing, or football or that. Anything but bloody work.

JIMMY: What do you put in your thermos this weather, Garretty?

GARRET: Lemonade, you daft bastard.

JIMMY: Then you could keep it in a bottle, and save your thermos for the winter. You'd save a fortune in refills.

SPOW: Your mother would save a fortune if she had your bloody head refilled.

[*Enter* HARRY *and* BAGLEY.]

BAGLEY: Hear you were spotted then, Wagsy.

WAGS: Yeah. Scouts from Birmingham City and Manchester United.

BAGLEY: I don't believe that.

WAGS: Believe what you like, but it's true. Scouts. They came to watch the opposing centre half, not me.

BAGLEY: Hadn't they heard of our Wagsy?

WAGS: No. They don't watch works teams.

BAGLEY: Why's that then?

WAGS: They think you're all tied up with your apprentice-ship.

HARRY: I like that. Tied, what do they think we are? Prisoners?

BAGLEY: I feel it in this heat. I had a look at the flesh under all this the other day. Repulsive. Like melted cheese. That French stuff.

DICKER: Wensleydale.

BAGLEY: That's the stuff. With bits of tomato in, that's my skin. You'll be all right, you'll be under bloody sun-ray treatment.

WAGS: We get all that.

HARRY: How did you shine out then, Wags?

BAGLEY: Natural talent.

WAGS: I knew they were looking at their centre half like, and he was looking good against our centre forward. I was playing on the wing, old-fashioned! Our team has the tactics of bloody Julius Caesar. I said to the captain, that big centre lathe turner from B shed, 'I want to play the four-two-four' and he said, 'You'll play on the wing like and get knotted,' so I thought, 'This is no good to me. They're stifling my talent. I'm a natural link man.' But there's no link man in our team.

BAGLEY: No idea of modern football.

WAGS: So I went and linked up. I kept pulling the ball out of the defence, dribbling midfield, like United, and luring the big daft centre half.

BAGLEY: Big, was he?

DICKER: Wags made him look like a carthorse. I was there.

WAGS: He was good in the air.

DICKER: So Wags kept it low. He just brought it down, and took it in low.

WAGS: The centre half came over to me at half time . . .

BAGLEY: What a sportsman.

WAGS: And said, 'Leave me alone or I'll screw you in the second half.'

DICKER: He didn't leave him alone, though. He took it to him all the time.

WAGS: The scouts both came up to me, and said they'd see my father about offering terms.

DICKER: Come on, Wags, try a shot.

[*They canter off.*]

BAGLEY: Offering terms? I hadn't thought of this before. We're prisoners. We're offered terms to get out. Wags is escaping.

HARRY: Fulcher's gone in the army. He got in the paratroopers. Free falling.

BAGLEY: Even Fulcher. Now Wags, trotting out at Old Trafford.

HARRY: Fulcher is on basic now. They reckon he injured the judo instructor.

BAGLEY: Did he? That's bad news for the Bagley. Who is the 'they' who 'reckoned'?

HARRY: I don't know. It could be Fulcher. Here's your girl. Have you told her about the St Ives trip?

BAGLEY: I'm getting round to it.

HARRY: Are you sure it's on?

BAGLEY [*gangsterwise*]: Don't you trust me, boy? Think I'm a bum? Think I'd double-cross yer, kid?

HARRY: You're double-crossing her.

BAGLEY: She's a broad, ain't she? Look, Harry, we're going. We're going to be footloose. We're off. I'm going to get my toes in the pebbles at St Ives and let the sea air get to my athlete's foot.

HARRY: She's waiting for you.

BAGLEY: I got her trained.

HARRY: Like that, is it?

BAGLEY: Begging for it.

HARRY: How do you do it?

BAGLEY: I must be endowed.

HARRY: You're not a prisoner there.

BAGLEY: And it's staying that way, kid. [*Ambles off.*]

HARRY: What you reading, Jeff?

JEFF: Third Year Calculus.

HARRY: Third Year? You mean you've been here for three years?

JEFF: That's it.

HARRY: And you've passed every year? You've never fallen at the fences?

JEFF: Yes. This is for next year's work. Advanced.

HARRY: Advanced? You're in the deep end. We dived in, for the first month this year. Me and Doug. But it was too near the Billiard Hall. We kept dropping in to pot the red, and before we knew where we were it was all over.

JEFF: You've got to keep your head down.

HARRY: How long will it be before you've got your certificates? You'll have chitties to frame and hang on the wall?

JEFF: I've got the little chitties framed now. Two years, all going well, I'll have my full certificate. Higher Certificate and Endorsements.

HARRY: Endorsements?

JEFF: They get you into the Institute of Engineers. It's a good thing to get your certificate endorsed.

HARRY: Jesus, I've got nothing.

JEFF: Never too late to start.

HARRY: This weather.

JEFF: After the holidays. Start.

HARRY: Me? Back to the beginning? It would be gruelling. Three nights a week out of my life.

JEFF: It's harder as you get older.

HARRY: You mean the brain cakes up? But look, I'm in the Billiards Team.

JEFF: Spow is Billiards Champion.

HARRY: It's a thought.

JEFF: It's all right, once you get into the habit of it. Jimmy there has passed his preliminaries.

HARRY: Jimmy has! What the hell was that for? Spelling?

JEFF: He isn't so daft. Just a slow starter.

HARRY: Slow starter. I thought he'd never started.

JEFF: He's started now. Haven't you, Jimmy?

JIMMY: What?

JEFF: You've started. Now you've passed your preliminary year, you've started.

JIMMY: Yeah. I passed. I got credits in sheet metal practical work. And I just passed the maths and mechanical drawing. I used to get sweaty under my tee square, you see, but Jeff here told me to take a rag in and wipe it. And I did. And passed.

HARRY: What a tip. The world is open to you now then, Jimmy?

JIMMY: Sure it is. I want to go in the drawing office line like Jeff.

HARRY: Drawing office, Jeff?

JEFF: Sure. I'm not staying in this yard all my life.
    [*Enter* RAMROD.]

RAMROD: Where is he? Where's my team?

JIMMY: Coming, Ramrod.

RAMROD: Get down there. I want you to do ten press ups.

JIMMY: I can only do eight.

RAMROD: Do eight then, then rest, then do the remainder to make ten. How many will that be?

JIMMY: Two.

RAMROD: Good lad. Any more for next season's team? Come on, soon be Olympic year.

SPOW: How's he shaping then, Ramrod? Daft Jimmy?

RAMROD: He's not bad. He's got a reach.

GARRET: It's about all he has got. It would be put to better use painting the ceiling.

RAMROD: He'll develop. Any more?

JIMMY: Ramrod.

RAMROD: I thought you were pressing up?

JIMMY: My mate wants to join next season.

RAMROD: That's good. All welcome. Who is it?

JIMMY: Him. Hi, Boswell. Here. I've asked.

BOSWELL: I'll join.

RAMROD: Yes. Well, son. I know about you. Have you brought a doctor's note?

BOSWELL: No, I'm all right.

RAMROD: Bring a doctor's note, son. Then you can join. I insist on doctor's notes.

BOSWELL: I'll try and get one.

RAMROD: You do that, son. Jimmy, in you get.

SPOW: You're like a father to them, Ramrod.

RAMROD: I know what it is to box much too early. It's worse than bloody shell-shock, I can tell you. That lad there, got a skull like a bantam's egg. I wouldn't put him in. Not without a doctor's note. Then I'd need a second opinion.

GARRET: Not daft Jimmy?

RAMROD: I'm bringing him on slowly. I put him in the ring sometimes with that berk from the packing shed, with sixteen ounce gloves and foam rubber on the floor; after ten seconds they just stand looking at each other. Haven't got the strength to keep their gum shields in. But he'll develop. Jimmy will develop. [*He goes.*]

GARRET: He's kind to them. He brings them on slowly.

SPOW: Hi, Wags, you ought to have somebody to bring your football on slowly, like Ramrod brings the boxers on.

DICKER: I'm bringing him on.

SPOW: You couldn't bring a kettle to the boil.

HARRY (*to* JEFF): Things going well, five years from now, Jimmy could be the clean-cut amateur champion of the drawing office.

JEFF: He's a sticker.

HARRY: And me, I'll be the boozed up champion of the Mason's Arms Snooker Hall. I might change.

JEFF: When?

HARRY: After the holidays. Provided me and Doug don't go Bohemian.

[BAGLEY *and* ALICIA.]

ALICIA: Are you trying to put me off then? Is that it?

BAGLEY: It isn't it. I'm going out with the lads, boozing.

ALICIA: I thought you were getting above all that.

BAGLEY: Did you? There's only one thing I can get above, love.

ALICIA: Don't talk like that, Douglas. Don't try and humiliate me.

BAGLEY: I'm not humiliating you.

ALICIA: You think I'm crawling after you, don't you?

BAGLEY: I don't see your knees worn out.

ALICIA: My mother's going to have the last word after all, I can see it.

BAGLEY: Well, what you going to do?

ALICIA: There's nothing for me to do, is there?

BAGLEY: You had a wild life before I came along, Young Conservatives, tennis, nude bathing and all that, sports car rallies. You can drop into all that again.

ALICIA: I'll stay in the house till you call.

BAGLEY: Well, all right then.

ALICIA: It's not too late, you know, Douglas. For the holidays.

BAGLEY: I've told you. I'm going camping with Harry. St Ives.

ALICIA: And I've got to tell my mother now that I'm not going with Harriet on the club trip. The lies I told to get away with you for the fortnight.

BAGLEY: You shouldn't have been telling lies. Your house is unbearable, like walking on glass. I'm frightened to be let alone with your mother, in case I put my foot in it with a load of counter lies and contradictions.

ALICIA: It's all right if you just behave sensible.

BAGLEY: I can't carry on that sort of conversation. I find it a strain. All this, 'If I say to her that Harriet was at the Con Club, when really Gregory and William had taken Margaret to the rally, and I should have been at the fête with flipping Samuel, then if Whit Sunday falls on the tenth I'm pommelled up to the arse in trouble.' I tell you, I don't know where I am. But I'm going to St Ives.

ALICIA: I'll see you in a fortnight then.

BAGLEY: Sure.

ALICIA: Just like that. Just like that.

BAGLEY: Just like that.

ALICIA: If I'm still here. [*She goes.*]

BAGLEY: Harry. Harry. I've gone and broke her heart.

HARRY: Bad as that?

BAGLEY: Terrible. I told her we were going to St Ives.

HARRY: It's on then?

BAGLEY: Bloody is on. Tent, you and me, mouth organ, hair long, jeans, beatniks, female beatniks; boy, we're roadsters. I'd even pick peas.

HARRY: I'm glad it's on.

BAGLEY: I tell you, she's a lovely girl. I like the girl. If she wasn't so mad about me I'd probably love her. I just won't take her. I want to get away. The strain has been too much. I did my best. All that Chinese food I ate, white wine, house-trained dog, all them plastic ducks; sitting in the parlour with Mam and Dad holding in a fart for three hours.

HARRY: You mean you did?

BAGLEY: I don't understand it. I don't understand it. I just don't get it, Harry. Hi, Wags, give us a kick of that ball.

WAGS: Steady, Doug, keep it low.

BAGLEY: I'm going to put a drop shot right through the typists' pool. Cause a splash.

DICKER: Keep it down, Doug. Use some science.

TAFFY: There is neither art nor science in soccer.

WAGS: You what?

TAFFY: Look at him, you'd think I'd just committed sacrilege in Liverpool Cathedral. Spit through the grille at the confessional.

DICKER: Keep his religion out of it, Taffy. He's Irish Liverpool.

TAFFY: What a mixture. Shamrock and scouse, no wonder they need Welsh lakes for their reservoirs.

WAGS: What did you say about football?

TAFFY: Any predictable fool can chase a round ball;

but only a man with initiative can play rugby football, rugby football.

WAGS: As far as I can see, it's just a matter of picking up a ball and running.

TAFFY: That's as far as you can see.

DICKER: He's going to turn professional.

TAFFY: I've heard different from his Dad in the club.

WAGS: He was sober.

TAFFY: He was drunk.

WAGS: And he said that? That's bad.

DICKER: He'll think different when Matt Busby comes round to your house.

TAFFY: Richard Burton came round to our house every day, back in Wales, but I didn't end up on the yacht.
   [BAGLEY and HARRY.]

BAGLEY: Look at them against the wall. Wonder where they're going for their holidays?

HARRY: They take their thermos flask on picnics.

BAGLEY: It's this heat. This shouldn't be allowed. Working in this heat. We should be on the East Coast, spinning for mackerel.

SPOW: Have you ever spun for mackerel then, Bagley?

BAGLEY: Listen to this. The walls have bloody ears here. Just stick your snout in that thermos and mind your tune.

GARRET: You kids, you're all blather, never spun for mackerel, have you?

BAGLEY: We have.

SPOW: You're lying.

BAGLEY: You've never spun for mackerel either.

SPOW: Never spun for mackerel? We go fishing every week-end, that's why we're so sexy.

BAGLEY: You sexy? That must be some bloody mackerel.

GARRET: You kids know nothing. We go every week-end. Bridlington.

HARRY: Brid? You go to Brid every week-end?

GARRET: 'Course we go to bloody Brid every week-end. We fix a boat up with the fishermen, and go off. Every week-end. Bring back a plastic bag full of fish.

BAGLEY: I didn't know you had a life outside of here.

SPOW: You kids don't know your arse from a hole in the ground.

BAGLEY: I tell you this, we're going away this fortnight. See that motorway, we'll be on it, we'll be going. Rule of thumb, man. Kipping out, roughing it. None of your thermos flask week-ends in Brid. [*Bagley and Harry move away.*] I didn't know they went to Brid.

HARRY: I thought they just propped the wall up every week-end.

BAGLEY: What do you do after a day's fishing?

SPOW: Go on the booze.

BAGLEY: How much does that sort of week-end cost you?

SPOW: There's no change from a fiver.

BAGLEY: I thought they went home every week-end and handed their packet over to their wives.

HARRY: Seemingly not!

BAGLEY: Look at Boswell. Don't say he's touching up Mabel? I mean, I've heard of spring in the air, but with her you'd need lightning. Let's squat, and enjoy the heat. What you doing?

HARRY: I'm opening up my shirt to let the sun at it.

BAGLEY: Futile vanity. You may as well put a coat of varnish on a frog's belly. Just wait till we get away though. St Ives, where the artists are, and the thinkers, lying on the sea wall, being rebellious, mebbe we'll pick up some guitar playing itinerants like ourselves and sing these bloody folk-songs. We might even buy a mouth organ, Harry, before we go, and tune up on the M.5.

    [BOSWELL *and* MABEL.]

BOSWELL: Did you say your name was Mabel?

MABEL: Yes.

BOSWELL: They're your friends over there, aren't they?

MABEL: Yes.

BOSWELL: Are they not close?

MABEL: No.

BOSWELL: You don't like people to be too close, do you?

MABEL: No.

BOSWELL: You work the sheet cutting machine, don't you?

MABEL: Yes.

BOSWELL: Good work, that. Heavy on the legs though. Do you find it heavy on the legs?

MABEL: Yes.

BOSWELL: My sister was a typist. Not like these here, she was better. She was a secretary, for company directors. She saved her legs. She went to school till she was eighteen. Gregg Shorthand. She could have gone on. But she broke.

MABEL: Did she?

BOSWELL: It was the strain. Getting up to her speeds.

MABEL: Speeds?

BOSWELL: Shorthand. She had to go away for a time. I was going to stay at school till I was eighteen, but my mother thought there shouldn't be two in the family and I came out. I like it here. I used to be shy. But I like it here. Bagley and that. It's communal like. You've got to say that. Communal. Is that why you like it?

MABEL: Yes.

[BAGLEY *and* HARRY.]

BAGLEY: Watching Boswell is making me randy.

HARRY: I think he's going to try and hold her hand.

BAGLEY: Let's go over and join the lassies. [*They go over to the girls.*] Hya, girls. It's been a long hot summer.

BETTY: He's got such a sure air of conversation.

BAGLEY: Where you going for your holidays?

BETTY: You being serious?

HARRY: Yes. We can be serious.

BAGLEY [*putting his hands round* BETTY'S *neck*]: Where you going, love?

BETTY: We're booked up for the south-west.

BAGLEY: What part?

BETTY: Ilfracombe.

BAGLEY: That's not the south-west, that's Bristol, the real happenings are further down. St Ives.

BETTY: We know that, but it's too far to go.

HARRY: Why too far?

LINDA: The train journey is murder. Ilfracombe is far enough.

BAGLEY: You should hitch-hike.

BETTY: It's all right for you. Boys.

BAGLEY: It's easier for girls. Just wave your pants.

LINDA: We thought we'd just go to Ilfracombe. It's nice there. Some of the artists and students get there.

BAGLEY: I tell you both, they're all at St Ives. Under canvas, or under the stars. It's warmer there, and the light is good.

HARRY: The light is like the Channel Isles. That's why the painters go.

BAGLEY: Painters, students, sculptors, writers, all of that. They all go.

BETTY: We know, we wanted to go, but we decided on Ilfracombe.

BAGLEY: Come with us.

BETTY: Pooh, with you.

BAGLEY: Seriously, love. You could come with us.

BETTY: But we've put a deposit down at the hotel.

BAGLEY: You would save that on train fare if you came with us. Hitch-hiking.

BETTY: But it's all organized.

BAGLEY: Ours is all disorganized. We're just upping and going, thumbs up, like Donovan and Bob Dylan.

[*They sing a snatch of travelling song.*]

BETTY: It sounds smashing. We fancied it, didn't we Linda.

LINDA: Yes. Everybody goes to St Ives who wants to be different.

HARRY: They reckon the characters there are all fantastic. There was a picture of them in the papers last year, sitting on the sea wall jeering at the Council attendants.

BAGLEY: They're a real rebellious mob. They're . . . like . . . philosophers, they don't believe in politics or owt like that.

LINDA: I've read about that.

HARRY: Like, they don't believe in organized religion or any of that. And they believe that everything should be free in society and that everybody should help everybody else, and they go round begging their food.

BAGLEY: It'll be great. Say you'll come.

BETTY: But where would we sleep?

BAGLEY: We can get you spare sleeping bags.

BETTY: How many tents have you got?

BAGLEY: One.

BETTY: But what about your typist?

BAGLEY: Don't be personal.

HARRY: Say you'll come then.

BETTY: It depends on Linda.

LINDA: I don't know.

BETTY: I don't mind, for myself like. Are you serious? Honest?

BAGLEY: Honest. You'd be all right, Linda, with Harry. Eh, Harry?

HARRY: Well, we'll all be together.

BAGLEY: Thrown together. Look, if you're going to be like that, we'll borrow another tent.

BETTY: Well? What do you think, Linda?

LINDA: Well, if you don't mind losing your deposit, Betty.

BAGLEY: You're a bit tight, aren't you, love?

BETTY: I don't mind. Honestly. Are you serious, Doug?

BAGLEY: Yes. Course I am. I'm not having you on. And Harry would love it, wouldn't you, Harry?

HARRY: Yes. Love it.

BETTY: All right then. I'll have to tell my mother.

LINDA: Me too.

BAGLEY: Bring them, we'll bring Spow and Garret.

[Hooter goes. Girls go.]

BAGLEY: Oy, Harry. What a body. I knew as soon as I put my hands round her. She stuck her body into me. No bloody false modesty there, no self sacrifice. No virgin tears.

HARRY: That would be hard.

BAGLEY: She just wanted it. I looked into her face at her cracked lipstick. I could see how it would be at St Ives. A bit of give and take; a friendly tussle over it. None of the tragic little dramas me and Alicia have been through on the tennis court seat. She's like a bloody animal after it. What a bitch. She's got a hell of a name, Harry; what a cow. Harry. I think I'm in love. Bags I last to clock on. Go on, you first. Stop trailing your feet.

[BAGLEY *and* HARRY *exit singing travelling song.*]

ACT TWO

SCENE ONE

After St Ives.

[WAGS *and* DICKER. SPOW *and* GARRET.]

SPOW: Back again. Back again. Can you not do without a ball at your toes?

GARRET: That ball sees more of his feet than his socks do.

DICKER: Move over then.

GARRET: It's still the cricket season. You ought to get some wickets chalked up on the wall.

WAGS: Cricket! Cricket! They only play that in floods.

SPOW: Bloody gentleman's game, that. Not like your football. Any hooligan can play football.

WAGS: Don't talk daft. Bobby Charlton was voted gentleman of the year.

TAFFY: Who by, his big brother?

[*Enter* BAGLEY.]

BAGLEY: Pass, pass, set me up a shot.

DICKER: Try this.

BAGLEY: You should have seen me on the sand at St Ives. The bloody demon rebel. Hair streaming down to my shoulders. A sort of penniless Rolling Stone. I was the only beatnik with a bit of football skill. Have you had your trial yet then, Wags?

WAGS: I'm getting a trial. I can't wait to get on a full-sized pitch.

DICKER: That's what he needs, my boy. A full-sized pitch.

WAGS: *And* a bit of decent turf. I'm sick of playing on the ash heaps round here.

DICKER: He needs a bit of decent turf.

WAGS: And to play with players of my own class, see. Instead of the big centre half from the Bronze Foundry.

DICKER: He needs players of his own class.

SPOW: He doesn't need a bloody ventriloquist's dummy.

[*Enter* JEFF *with* LEO, *a coloured boy.*]

GARRET: Hi, Taffy, one of your pack of cards got loose. Ace of Spades.

JEFF: All right, you can carry on smoking.

BAGLEY: Who's the lad, Jeff?

JEFF: He's Leo, Leo James.

HARRY: Is he come to see where the slaves are quartered?

JEFF: He's come to work here.

SPOW: He must be semi-skilled. They're taking on semi-skilled.

BAGLEY: Where do you come from then, Leo?

LEO: Dominica, in the Windward Islands.

HARRY: The Windward Islands, that's where the pirates were.

SPOW: That's where they cut the sugar-cane.

VOICES: Aw shut up, you. Don't show your ignorance. Less of that, Spow.

BAGLEY: We had to have one voice in the corner, didn't we, Enoch?

SPOW: I just said it's where the sugar-cane comes from.

LEO: And it is, we have the biggest sugar-cane refinery in the world out there, and proud of the fact.

SPOW: There, I told you. Race conscious bastards, think only the young has tolerance.

BAGLEY: Oh. You aren't an apprentice then, Leo?

LEO: I'm a graduate apprentice.

HARRY: What does that mean?

LEO: I have my degree, I am coming to serve two years as a fitter, to get to know the trade from the inside.

JIMMY: We're different, we learn the trade first, then go to university.

HARRY: To mend the plumbing.

BAGLEY: Does that mean you have letters after your name then, Leo?

LEO: Yes. B.Sc.

BAGLEY: B.Sc! Anyway kid, make this prison your home ... it might not be the Windward Islands, but the canteen does sell coconut bars ... hi, did you get your degree in a cap and gown?

LEO: Yes.

BAGLEY: Over your overalls? I'd love to have seen that.

TAFFY: The biggest stroke of democracy since Keir Hardie took his seat in Parliament in a cloth cap.

BAGLEY: Make yourself at home. Taffy, make the lad at home, you've both come from overseas ... not much difference between you and him, especially down the pit with you speaking Welsh. Come on, lads, let football commence.

[*Enter* MR BRADBURY.]

MR BRADBURY: Watch it, Bagley, Mr Raines has his eye on you.

BAGLEY: Oh, yes. Better play at top end, lads.

[*Exit* BAGLEY *and footballers.*]

TAFFY: Old Bagley has got very broadminded. Not that I'm complaining, but he's got very broadminded.

HARRY: He's been opened out, see, there was stacks of wogs at St Ives.

GARRET: They've been to St Ives, you'd think they'd been round the world.

HARRY: The world *is* at St Ives Garret. That's where the world is. In the summer.

DICKER: Where have you been then, Spow?

SPOW: You wouldn't know where it is.

HARRY: Name it.

SPOW: Spern Point.

HARRY: Spern Point?

SPOW: You wouldn't know where it is.

HARRY: What's so good at Spern Point?

GARRET: Tell him.

SPOW: It's the finest plaice fishing in the world at the right time of year.

DICKER: Plaice fishing? Plaice fishing? I gave up fishing years ago.

SPOW: That was in the canal with maggots and a jam jar.

GARRET: We're talking about the real fishing. Plaice, finest sport, and finest food in the world.

DICKER: What a holiday. Plaice fishing. Off the end of the pier.

SPOW: Off a boat, mate.

DICKER: Rowing boat? Or gravy boat?

SPOW: Keel boat, mate. A trawler. That's what we were off. Bloody St Ives.

HARRY: Where's Spern Point?

SPOW: Off the Humber. Ignorant.

HARRY: Do you see big boats off the Humber?

GARRET: Of course we do, we fish in the shipping lanes.

HARRY: Shipping lanes? Can you reach the shipping lanes?

SPOW: They're only a few miles out. None of your real deep sea stuff like St Ives, but we see the odd tanker, or Flat Iron or cargo boat.

HARRY: That sounds great. I wouldn't mind the Merchant Navy. Think I could get to sea from here?

GARRET: If you walk far enough you'll drop in.

SPOW: Pakistanis are landing on the coast of Kent every day out of cabin cruisers, surely *you* can get to sea?

GARRET: Nelson managed. Without free milk.

HARRY: I'd like to get in.

[JEFF *and* LEO.]

JEFF: Is your B.Sc. as high as you'll go now you're in the shop, Leo?

LEO: No. After two years here I'll qualify for my doctor of science.

JEFF: I'm just on the technological courses. It's more practical I suppose than the degree course.

LEO: That doesn't matter, you'll be able to transfer to a degree course after that.

JEFF: I'll give the firm that, they'll push you as far as you can take it. But degree course – I doubt if I could make that.

LEO: You will, if you get your diploma.

JEFF: I'd like to be a travelling engineer, going abroad

with the gear, installing, supervising, I wouldn't mind maintenance if I could travel. I'd like that. But the firm likes its men abroad to be in the Institute of Engineers.

LEO: I want to qualify for the Institute before I go back.

JEFF: But you'll need your degree, this doctorate, the lot?

LEO: Yes. The lot.

JEFF: I just went to Secondary School.

LEO: That doesn't matter.

JEFF: Whenever I think clearly of what I'm trying to do, I sometimes think I'll lose my nerve. It all seems too big. Still, it could have been worse.

[MABEL *and* BOSWELL.]

BOSWELL: It's not bad. Is it? Being back?

MABEL: I don't mind it.

BOSWELL: Did you go away?

MABEL: Only for two days.

BOSWELL: Days is all right. Day trips?

MABEL: My mother said, we wouldn't go away, just on day trips.

BOSWELL: Well, it's cheaper, and it's quick. And you can have a bed to come back to.

MABEL: That's what my mother said. About a bed to come back to.

BOSWELL: You don't have to bother about hotels, on day trips.

MABEL: That's why we went on day trips.

BOSWELL: And there's plenty to see round here, the Derbyshire Dales, and things. Stately Homes. Belle Vue.

MABEL: They run a smashing trip to the Derbyshire Dales.

BOSWELL: Yes. And did you just book up and go? Just like that?

MABEL: Yes.

BOSWELL: Fancy free.

MABEL: Yes.

BOSWELL: You can cram a lot into a fortnight.

MABEL: Well, you can, going dailies. And you don't have to decide till the last minute.

BOSWELL: Where did you go to?

MABEL: We had a day in the Derbyshire Dales.

BOSWELL: Anywhere else?

MABEL: We were going to go to a Stately Home, but my mother said it wears you off your feet going round Stately Homes.

BOSWELL: It does. It does. Going round Stately Homes.

MABEL: So we didn't go.

BOSWELL: Did you go on any other day trips?

MABEL: We didn't fancy Belle Vue. The smell and the crowds.

BOSWELL: There are good day trips from here.

[*Enter* RAMROD.]

RAMROD: Is there anybody for the boxing team this year? Anybody at all from this shed?

JIMMY: Me, Ramrod. But I want to be entered for competitions.

RAMROD: All right, son, I'll take your name.

JIMMY: You know my name.

RAMROD: But I take it fresh each year. Any more names? Come on, gels. Bagley, can I put you down for the boxing team?

BAGLEY: I'm non-violence.

SPOW: That makes a change.

GARRET: It was all them bleedin' beatniks.

RAMROD: Is there nobody else for the boxing then? What can you do with them? Mr Raines has promised us track suits this year if we get a good team together.

HARRY: Second-hand boiler suits they'll be.

RAMROD: With the firm's motifs on the back.

JIMMY: Like Cadbury's. At the championships.

RAMROD: They had all the equipment, Cadbury's did, when they entered for the tournament. Chocolate shorts, with white vests and milk chocolate neckbands. Smashing they looked.

BAGLEY: We'll have the sign of the golden rivet.

LEO: Sir, I think I'd like to join your team.

TAFFY: Hear that? Sir.

WAGS: These coloured boys are sportsmen, and they got manners.

SPOW: When they want something.

LEO: Say, sir, I'd like to join the boxing.

RAMROD: Son, did I hear right?

LEO: I'd like to join. I've done a bit.

RAMROD: Now isn't that something. This lad has come all the way from . . . where you from son?

LEO: Wolverhampton.

RAMROD: Before that, before that?

LEO: Notting Hill Gate.

RAMROD: This lad's father has come all the way here from Africa, and you lot is shown up. Are you not ashamed of yourselves?

VOICES: Aw, Ramrod. We'd have joined. We're no good, Ramrod. We're excused boxing.

RAMROD: Right, son. You look good. I'll make a boxer of you. What weight are you?

LEO: Twelve half.

RAMROD: Twelve and a half, and all muscles. Right, come on, come on, Jimmy.

[*They go.*]

BAGLEY: That's given you a fright, Spow. I'm glad I'm his mate.

WAGS: Fine sportsmen, these coloured fellers.

DICKER: They're the best. There was one at Wimbledon this year.

WAGS: They're good at cricket, too.

BOSWELL: Look at the West Indies.

BAGLEY: And running. Running, you can't see the black bastards over a hundred yards. I meant that friendly, Spow.

WAGS: And Pele, Pele is the world's greatest goal scorer.

DICKER: And long jumping.

BOSWELL: Look at Cassius.

GARRET: Bloody hell. It's friends of Biafra week, this. Why don't you sell flags outside the gate?

SPOW: The way they feel now they'd turn black themselves, given the chance.

VOICES: They're fine fellers. Good blokes, the coloureds. Real sports.

SPOW: You'll be whistling a different tune when they start screwing your daughters.

[LINDA *to* JEFF.]

LINDA: Hello, Jeff.

JEFF: Glad to see you back, Linda.

LINDA: Had a good holiday? Where have you been?

JEFF: Where have I been? Does that matter? Does it matter where *any* of us have been? I thought the St Ives gang were the only ones who'd *been* anywhere. I didn't think the rest of us were *alive*.

LINDA: Don't say that, Jeff. Where have you been?

JEFF: I went camping. With some of the lads.

LINDA: That's all we did.

JEFF: This wasn't hitch-hiking down the M.5. Meeting adventure where it knocked.

LINDA: What did you do? Go on your motor bike?

JEFF: Yes. I made a trailer. You know, I got a couple of wheels off an old chassis, made a frame, trailer. It's a good idea, a trailer.

LINDA: We lived rough, but ... we missed things ...

JEFF: Like?

LINDA: Stove, blankets, food, stuff like that. Where did you go, Jeff?

JEFF: Oh, we went about. The Hebrides was the furthest we got.

LINDA: The Hebrides? Are you being funny?

JEFF: No, we meant to go there, or Shetland.

BAGLEY: Hi, Linda, Linda, come here, will you?

JEFF: Your gang wants you.

BAGLEY: Come here, Linda, I want to ask you something.

LINDA: Don't shout. I can hear.

BAGLEY: Where's Bet?

LINDA: She's resting. After dinner.

BAGLEY: After dinner? Resting? God help us, don't say the St Ives trip made her that exhausted.

LINDA: She's just resting. That's all. Resting.

BAGLEY: Here's Alicia. She looks brown. Must have been under the infra red at the club. Harry, you look white.

HARRY: You're just an off yellow.

BAGLEY: That's what the sun does to me. Hello, Alicia.

ALICIA: Douglas. I can't stop. I'm in a hurry. For Mr Raines.

BAGLEY: Alicia. To hell with Mr Raines.

ALICIA: I'll be back in a minute, Douglas. I'm just in a hurry for Mr Raines. [*She goes.*]

BAGLEY: She's being middle class. She's playing hard to get.

HARRY: She had a message for Mr Raines.

BAGLEY: She can go running after Mr Raines for the rest of her life. I thought what we had was bigger than Mr Raines. She wouldn't know. She's got no sense of proportion.

HARRY: Perhaps she's offended.

BAGLEY: Offended. I can see she's offended.

LINDA: Douglas. Aren't you going to ask how Betty is?

BAGLEY: Sure. How is she?

LINDA: She's resting.

JIMMY: Where's your lass then, Bagley?

LINDA: She's just resting.

JIMMY: Where's your typist, Bagley?

BAGLEY: She's just passed by. Just gone.

SPOW: Where is she then, Bagley?

GARRET: Is she off with the lads up the drawing office, Bagley.

BAGLEY: There's a rush job on for Mr Raines. Can you not take a telling? The pencils up in the drawing office are red hot. She'll be back in a minute.

VOICES: Whoa. You've lost her, Bag. Back to the dance, Bag. You've missed your chance in society. She's had enough, Bag.

BAGLEY: She's coming back, I tell you. She's coming back.

[*Enter* ALICIA.]

ALICIA: Douglas. Douglas.

JIMMY: Somebody wants you, Bag.

BAGLEY: What's that? Oh. Hello, Alice. Here a minute, love.

ALICIA: That's right. Make me come to you.

BAGLEY: That was a cliffhanger. You came at the right moment.

ALICIA: I notice I had to come to you. Running.

BAGLEY: Never again, love. Never again. That was the last snap of my fingers, I can tell you.

ALICIA: What about St Ives?

BAGLEY: You go to St Ives, pet, and you'll find your name carved on every tree.

ALICIA: Lies.

BAGLEY: Well, it's near the truth.

ALICIA: I hear you had a great time.

BAGLEY: Yeah. It was great. It wasn't too bad for you, was it, Alice?

ALICIA: I went to the New Forest with Mam and Dad, they were taking the caravan, I went with them at the last minute.

BAGLEY: It's good down there, isn't it? The New Forest. Where is it?

ALICIA: It's on the South Coast. It is nice. Not St Ives, of course. Look, Mr Raines has us all on the run. Honest. I'll try and get back before the buzzer goes.

BAGLEY: What about your lunch break?

ALICIA: Mr Raines has asked us to stagger lunches so that we don't clash with the factory.

BAGLEY: Try to get back then.

[*She is about to go.*]

LINDA: Bagley, Betty hasn't come from dinner. She thought you might be going in.

ALICIA: See you then, Douglas.

BAGLEY: See you.

LINDA: It's not very nice, Douglas.

BAGLEY: It's not very nice, Douglas. Hi, where's the New Forest? Anybody know where the New Forest is?

BOSWELL: Wales. I think.

TAFFY: Is it hell in Wales.

BOSWELL: I thought it was in Wales. Down the Wye Valley?

TAFFY: What's he talking about? The New Forest was planted by William the Conqueror.

BAGLEY: I don't want to know who planted it. Where is it?

TAFFY: It's in Hampshire.

BAGLEY: I'm none the wiser.

GARRET: The St Ives bus didn't go past it.

[*Enter* MR BRADBURY *in new white overalls. Uproar.*]

BAGLEY: What have they done to you, Mr Bradbury?

DICKER: Are you a monk, Mr Bradbury?

HARRY: Do you have to turn celibate?

SPOW: Taffy. He's off to the Eisteddfod.

BAGLEY: You look like a nun, Mr Bradbury. Nun but the purest.

HARRY: I bet Mr Raines loves him in that.

BAGLEY: Don't talk like that, he's virgin white.

SPOW: Take no notice of them, Mr Bradbury?

MR BRADBURY: I'm bloody not.

GARRET: That's the best way to deal with them.

BAGLEY: Now Mr Bradbury bowls from the Gas Tank end, the turf is beautifully green, and he comes, with his run up, just a trace of hip movement, a mere nicety, nothing you can accuse him of, he bowls a maiden over.

MR BRADBURY: One of these days it'll happen to you.

BAGLEY [*nancy like*]: Oh, I shouldn't think so, Mr Bradbury.

MR BRADBURY: One of these days, it'll bloody happen to you. The factory is modernizing. We're changing from A.C. to D.C. and turning the lubricators over to diesel, soon we'll *all* be in white.

BAGLEY: They'll never get me in white.

BRADBURY: Never is a long time, Bagley.
[*He goes. They all whistle ' Here comes the Bride'.*]
[*Enter* ALICIA. DOUGLAS *to her.*]

BAGLEY: Was it miserable down in the New Forest? I suppose it was all rounders in the clearing, wasn't it?

ALICIA: Well, for some. But Rodney came.

BAGLEY: Rodney?

ALICIA: I didn't know he wanted to come. That night you went to St Ives, he came to our house, hinted about the New Forest ponies . . .

BAGLEY: Trust him to know his geography.

ALICIA: So, we took him along. I really got to know him. Mam and Dad were nice, they threw us together a bit, you know how they are.

BAGLEY: Can't say I noticed them throwing me and you together.

ALICIA: Well, in a caravan. What can you expect? They went off for days. Left Rodney and I. In the caravan. Or we went off for days.

BAGLEY: And left them in the caravan? Had a sexy week, the lot of you.

ALICIA: We had a very nice time. Time flew.

BAGLEY: That's a good sign.

ALICIA: So, that's how it is.

BAGLEY: I feel put out.

ALICIA: You might, for a day or two.

BAGLEY: But it's not all off . . . or on?

ALICIA: As you say, Douglas. Nothing definite. You never really got to know Rodney, did you?

BAGLEY: No.

ALICIA: He's very nice.

BAGLEY: I'm sure he is. You'll have to invite me along one night.

ALICIA: Silly thing. Nothing definite. [*She goes.*]

WAGS [*to* DICKER]: I tell you what. I wouldn't stay with Manchester if they started slipping.

DICKER: Would you not?

WAGS: That I wouldn't. I'd be out. Get to a top team.

TAFFY: Somebody ought to let Matt Busby know, his plans are in jeopardy.

GARRET: If he's going to play for Manchester United, he'd better put some weight on. Skinny thing. Eat some good grub. Like fish, or sandwiches. If he plays like that he'll be strangled to death by a flying toilet roll.

WAGS: George Best's light.

SPOW: He's got my colour eyes but I can't play like him.

[Enter RAMROD, LEO and JIMMY.]

RAMROD: I've got a champ. I've got a champ.

TAFFY: That was quick.

RAMROD: I've got a champ in this boy. A champ.

TAFFY: I've heard of Instant Whipping but this is ridiculous.

RAMROD: This boy has grace, precision, he moves like a panther.

SPOW: He ought to, he looks like one.

RAMROD: I hope you boys are sorry for yourselves now, see. The works will be proud of the team, mark my words. Proud of the team, when this lad, these two lads get started.

GARRET: They're like the Black and White Minstrel Show.

JIMMY [to WAGS]: You're right, Wags. If you play with fellers of your own class, you come on a ton. I feel great already.

SPOW: Don't trip your bloody self up with your Ali shuffle.

BAGLEY [to HARRY]: Harry, I really think she is indifferent.

HARRY: What do you expect, leaving her to go to St Ives. Doug, I might try classes again this year.

BAGLEY: Oh, come on, classes. Where do you want to go?

HARRY: I haven't decided yet, Bag.

BAGLEY: Up in the drawing office? Is that what you're after? Leather patches on your elbows, and a shiny arse? Is that your ambition?

HARRY: Something like that. I don't know.

BAGLEY: Classes! How many of the St Ives hippies went to classes?

81

HARRY: How many of them went anywhere? They were mostly on holiday or on the dole.

BAGLEY: They were great characters, Harry. Nomads.

HARRY: Nomads! They were just like us, there to see somebody else looking like poets and painters and that.

BAGLEY: There was painters.

HARRY: Painters? I wouldn't turn them loose on our back door.

BAGLEY: That was their style.

HARRY: They'd plenty of that. Style. It's about all they had.

BAGLEY: Do you want to go back? Is that it? Me and you? I mean, you say the word kid, and we'll go back down to St Ives and be serious drifters. We'll not be just summer philosophers, we'll be winter, all the year round men, like Bob Dylan.

HARRY: Talk sense, Doug, Dylan lives in a hotel. He just puts his red muffler on and his Levis when he's hitch-hiking to the Carnegie Hall in his chauffeur-driven Chevvy.

BAGLEY: We should have stayed, Harry.

HARRY: What was the use? How many of them were real hippies? Sitting there, strumming their guitars. That bloody poet, with the ginger hair and Davy Crockett shirt, you know what he was? A glass-blower up in Leeds. And that gang who said they were hitch-hiking to Istanbul? They were getting back to Bolton, they worked in a wholesale clothing mail order firm; my mother gets their catalogue. Phoney, phoney, the whole thing. There wasn't an artist among the lot of them who could pass the extrance exam for Painting by Numbers College; that feller, the one with the Mexican hat, sitting there sketching to attract the birds, he couldn't draw teeth.

BAGLEY: He got the women though; I heard he painted them in the nude.

HARRY: He might have started.

BAGLEY: I think they were philosophers, the lot of them, all that discussion on the sands. When the rain stopped.

HARRY: They were all acting philosophers and artists

for a fortnight; I'm no connoisseur, but I know when I'm up to my ears in crap.

BAGLEY: Don't shake my beliefs, Harry, there's a long winter ahead.

HARRY: I saw one feller, couple of birds with him, sitting on the sea wall, flicking orange peel at the family groups on the sand, said he was existential. I got to know him. Bus conductor in London. Man, there wasn't a real one among the whole crew.

BAGLEY: You're getting very set in your ways.

HARRY: We're all set in our ways. I'm thinking how to get unset.

BAGLEY: So, what do we do?

HARRY: I'm not going to be a machine-minder all my life. Even if it does mean classes.

BAGLEY: You've lost your rebel instinct. They've got you, kid. But they haven't got me. I'll tell you that.

[*Hooter goes.*]

Bags I last one to clock on.

[*Enter* LINDA.]

LINDA: Douglas.

BAGLEY: Yeah?

LINDA: It isn't very nice, you know. Betty's been in the Rest Room all dinner time and you haven't been in to see her.

BAGLEY: What's she been doing in the Rest Room?

LINDA: Just resting. She's upset, you know. I wish you wouldn't be so inconsiderate.

BAGLEY: Well, I'll drop by and see her.

LINDA: Mr Raines said you should.

SCENE TWO

Marriage

[*All standing outside the office. Uproar.*]

ALL: We want Bag. We want Bag. We want Bag.

APPRENTICE: He's in with Mr Raines getting the office present.

ALL: We want Bag. We want Bag. We want Bag.

[BAGLEY *and* BETTY *come out of office. Big cheer.*]

APPRENTICE: Silence for the best man.

HARRY: Silence. Silence all. Well, this is a day not many of us expected to see in a hurry.

ALL: Whoah.

HARRY: They say that brides are getting younger every day but Bagley is ridiculous. He went fishing in St Ives but his catch pulled him in.

VOICE: Too much cod, Bagley.

HARRY: However, they're in it together now, sink or swim.

VOICE: The breast stroke Bagley.

HARRY: And I think I say, for all of us, it couldn't happen to a finer couple. We have all, at one time or other, felt Bagley's fist or tongue.

ALL: Booo.

HARRY: Both of which are foul and coated.

ALL: Hurray.

HARRY: But underneath that thick-skinned exterior there must beat a heart, because Betty claims she's found it.

BETTY: I have, I have.

HARRY: Without further ado ... speaking for myself, not the blissful pair. ... We had a whip round here, and when I say whip, brothers, it took some whipping to force the pennies out of some pockets in the cause.

BETTY: I don't believe it.

BOSWELL: It's not true neither, everybody gave.

HARRY: However, to the happy couple I offer this present,

it's well wrapped, like streaky bacon, I hope the string comes in useful.

ALL: Speech, speech.

BETTY: Have we to open it first?

ALL: Yes. Open it.

[*They open it. Loud 'Ahs' and 'Ohs'. A carry cot.*]

BETTY: Well, it's lovely. I can't thank you enough.

ALL: Speech. Speech, Bagley. Speech.

BAGLEY: Well, I think this present shows your usual grasp of the situation. I told you we'd bring a present back from St Ives, didn't I? Mind you, I was thinking more in terms of sticks of rock; but sticks of rock were hard to come by this year at St Ives.

ALL: Hooh.

BAGLEY: There's just the wedding to get over with now. It's in a church. St Mark's. You won't recognize it, most of you. But it's a big building with a point on top.

BOSWELL: It's a white wedding, Mabel.

BAGLEY: Don't let us down with your ignorance. Take your hats off inside. And Spow, don't take your thermos.

VOICE: Where you going for your honeymoon, Bagley?

BAGLEY: We won't tell you the exact address. But we're going to St Ives, for sentimental reasons. But this time, we'll sleep in a hotel, not on the beach, that sand gets in everywhere.

VOICE: And it does the trick.

BETTY: Oh, shut up. The vulgarity.

BAGLEY: Have I said too much?

VOICE: No. Go on Bagley.

BAGLEY: Well, when we get back I'll tell you all what married life's like, lads. But from the foretaste I've had it's intoxicating. If I like it I'm going to see Mr Raines about making it compulsory. We're having the reception in the Co-op Hall, it's a sit-down job, and Betty's mother's bought her dowry; fifty crates of brown ale, it's a good honeymoon brew.

[*All cheer. They throw confetti.*]

VOICE: How did Mr Raines take it, Bag?

BAGLEY: Oh, he was grand. Grand. Very nice indeed.

BETTY: He was lovely. And the office staff. All lovely. They gave us a lovely tea service.

VOICE: Working this afternoon, Bagley?

BAGLEY: That I'm not. I'm being fitted.

VOICES: Good luck then both. Good luck.

LINDA [*with transistor*]: It's on. It's on. Listen.

BOSWELL: Come on. It's a surprise. A request.

BAGLEY: What is it?

LINDA: A tune for you and Betty. Bob Miller and the Millermen.

JIMMY: He said, 'Congratulations to you, Bagley.'

BAGLEY: I don't know him.

DICKER: It's a Dylan number.

BAGLEY: Bloody Dylan. He still singing, is he?

BETTY: It's our St Ives tune, Douglas.

[*They listen the tune out.*]

WAGS: Hi, Bag, can I make an announcement?

BAGLEY: What's that?

WAGS: I might not be here when you get back.

BAGLEY: What's up then, Wags?

WAGS: I thought I'd keep it for a surprise, I'm getting my trial for Manchester United.

ALL: Good old Wags. Wags for United, Wags for United. Zigger Zagger, Zigger Zagger, we want Wags. Wags for United.

BAGLEY: Hi, Wags.

WAGS: What?

BAGLEY: How about a change? You go to St Ives, and I'll go to Old Trafford.

[*Hooter goes.*]

WAGS: Not on your life. Begging your pardon, Betty.

BAGLEY: Get back in. The lot of you. Bags I don't clock on at all.

[*They all go.* BETTY *and* BAGLEY *are left.*]

BETTY: You weren't serious, were you, Douglas.

BAGLEY: What about?

86

BETTY: You wouldn't change with him, would you? And go to Manchester?

BAGLEY: I wouldn't change with any of them, love.

BETTY: Honest?

[*They go.* BAGLEY *proudly. He has tins pinned on his coat.*]

BAGLEY: St Ives will be my Wembley in life.

SCENE THREE

Fulcher's Second Leap.

DICKER: Here, try this. Oh, it's murder without Wags.

SPOW: At least with that lot it won't go over the wall.

DICKER: Try a kick. Come on. Ignore them. I wish I was at Old Trafford today. I'd give a week's wages to be at Old Trafford.

GARRET: You couldn't get to Old Trafford on thirty bob a week.

DICKER: I've got no team left to train.

SPOW: You're like Alf Ramsey, when they won the World Cup they all dropped bloody dead with the effort.

DICKER: They beat the Germans.

SPOW: So did me and Garret but we get no thanks.

BOSWELL: Come on then, Dicker, pass up.

JIMMY: He wants to get a game in before Mabel comes out.

BOSWELL: Give us a header, give us a header.

DICKER: Better not, eh, Bos? With your head.

BOSWELL: It's not true, I tell you, it's not true.

DICKER: All the same. Better not. Rely on me, I trained Wags carefully.

SPOW: Anybody heard from Bagley? Before he went we were going to get a postcard every day from St Ives. Once he got his wedding present, he'd forgot.

HARRY: I've had one. He sends his love.

SPOW: Has he any left?

HARRY: He's coming back today. Said he'd drop in.

GARRET: What's he coming back today for? Sick of it?

SPOW: Has he had enough?

HARRY: The trains are better. They're murder on a Saturday and Sunday from St Ives.

GARRET: Trains! Like hell. He's sick of it already. Honeymoons are like that, though.

HARRY: Stop whispering, will you? Dirty buggers.

DICKER: Wish I was with Wags now. He said, if he ever gets on, he'll remember me. I'll carry his sponge or something.

HARRY: Is that what he said?

DICKER: Yeah, if he ever gets on, he'll remember me.

TAFFY: Hoh, that's a right tale. Anybody gets on forgets their mates, I can tell you. I lived next door to Richard Burton.

VOICES: You never. He never. Get on with the game. Ignore him. Richard Burton.

TAFFY: I lived next door to Richard bloody Burton, but I never get an invite to his yacht. I lived next door to Richard Burton. We went to the same school. We played in the same scrum. A good team that was, as well. We had Stanley Baker on the wing. I was in the second row. Richard was prop. We had Harry Secombe at fly-half, and my uncle Emlyn – you've heard of him, Emlyn Williams?

HARRY: Another Welsh gem.

TAFFY: Aye, well he used to come down sometimes at week-ends and referee. Well, it was Richard who broke that team up. A real shame – he was a first-class player. He'd have played for Wales if he'd kept going, but he threw it all over and went up to London to do the acting – a real shame. Anyway, when he was in Stratford acting the Shakespeare my Uncle Emlyn decided we should all go up to see him. So early one morning on Cardiff General there was Dylan –

HARRY: Who? Bob Dylan?

TAFFY: Thomas, you twit! Poetry! Anyway Dylan was there – but Dylan was always there – and Geraint Evans, Stanley Baker, Harry Secombe, myself, and there was little Cliff Morgan in his little peak cap and short trousers and my Uncle Emlyn and all. We all caught the early morning train – only not too early 'cause we had to wait for Donald Houston to finish the night shift down the mines. When we got there we caught two taxis to the theatre – 'cause there was so many of us. We sat through the Shakespeare and afterwards we went backstage and there was Richard all covered in grease paint and sweat and my Uncle Emlyn started to talk about Wales and our street and the pub and the chapel and the mines and so on and Richard said, 'That's all very well, but what about my performance?' And Dylan the poet said, 'It was magnificent' and Geraint the singer he said . . .

[TAFFY *breaks into a Welsh song, during which –*]:

BOSWELL: Is it French?

HARRY: No, it's German, I think. It's Russian.

TAFFY [*finishing song*]: It's Welsh, you twit! And little Cliff in his little peak cap and short trousers said, 'It's all very well, but it's not the same as playing rugby for Wales!

[TAFFY *laughs. The others remain silent.*]

HARRY: Yeah. So what happened then?

BOSWELL: I didn't know Richard Burton was Welsh.

JIMMY: I think he's having us on.

[*Enter* JEFF. HARRY *goes over to him.*]

HARRY: Hi, Jeff, where's Linda?

JEFF: She isn't out yet.

HARRY: She told me you were going in the drawing office. That right?

JEFF: Yes. I've been with Mr Raines, I do six months up there, then six months on the floor again, then I'm at the Tech.

HARRY: You'll get full-time release for your certificates?

JEFF: Yes. I'm on full-time release next year.

HARRY: Bet you're glad?

JEFF: It's a relief.

HARRY: Your brother went in the Merchant Navy, didn't he?

JEFF: That's right.

HARRY: Is he still in?

JEFF: Yes. Engineer.

HARRY: How did he do it?

JEFF: He went to Tech and got a diploma.

HARRY: All right, all right, all right. It all starts and ends with bloody diplomas, doesn't it?

JEFF: Well, it does, in this game.

HARRY: What's wrong with the old days where you just ran off to the quayside and worked your passage? Now you've got to have your cards and stamps and diplomas.

JEFF: That's how it is.

HARRY: Back to square one. It's like Ludo.

JEFF: Why this craze for the sea? Did you catch it at St Ives?

HARRY: Don't *you* start being funny about St Ives. I'm sick of the St Ives humorists.

JEFF: I wasn't being funny.

HARRY: Is there no other way of getting into the Navy?

JEFF: You could try the Royal Navy.

HARRY: What? In that uniform? Three stripes for Nelson, a shoulder piece to keep your tarred pigtail off your shirt, bell bottoms. I want to see the world; not show the flag in Plymouth.

JEFF: I don't know any other ways, Harry.

[*Enter* LINDA.]

LINDA: Hello, Harry.

HARRY: Hello, Linda.

LINDA: You're miserable. Missing Bagley?

HARRY: No.

JEFF: He wants to go to sea.

HARRY: Don't say it like that.

LINDA: Do you, though? Want to go to sea?

HARRY: Yes. I do. I'd like to. I've been thinking about it. But I don't want to sound like Captain Cook or Horatio Nelson. Merchant Navy.

LINDA: Speak to Mr Raines. He's very helpful.

HARRY: Mr Raines. Me? Speak to Mr Raines? Him?

LINDA: He was very nice over Bagley's marriage.

HARRY: What's that got to do with the Merchant Navy?

JEFF: Well, should I be moving off?

HARRY: No. You shouldn't. But I should.

[*Enter* FULCHER.]

FULCHER: Hi, still here, you lot? Still sitting about? Still sitting playing dominoes and cards? Cards, eh, Taffy?

TAFFY: We haven't all seen the world like you Fulch, Catterick.

FULCHER: I've been at Aldershot, mate. Training. Basics. We've been camping out. I was brown as a berry, but I lost it on the train coming up.

JIMMY: Where's your wings then, Fulch?

FULCHER: Haven't gone in for it yet. It's the most exclusive club in the world, the paras.

TAFFY: Is it hell. The Eisteddfod is.

FULCHER: That's for Druids. But if you're not a Druid the paras is. Hi, Harry, he's coming back isn't he?

HARRY: Who?

FULCHER: Bagley. I'm after him. Bagley, when is he coming back?

HARRY: It's not fair. He's on his honeymoon.

FULCHER: I know where he is, when's he coming back.

HARRY: It's not fair. You're trained. You're a professional.

FULCHER: That's his big worry.

JIMMY: I hear you injured the judo instructor, Fulch.

FULCHER: Yeah, and he was a Fourth Dan. Black belt.

JIMMY: Poor Bagley. My boxing's coming on.

FULCHER: Boxing's hopeless. No boxing could stand up against a karate. You're a boxer, try me with a straight left.

JIMMY: No, I'm not. Why should I? I'm not mixing it with a karate.

FULCHER: How long you been boxing?

JIMMY: Eight months.

FULCHER: I've only been doing karate for two months but I could kill you.

JIMMY: You could before you started.

FULCHER: I'll train you if you like. When you get sick of the boxing. I'll train you. Falling first. You've got to know how to fall. Watch this and I'll show you how to fall. Breakfall they call it. Watch.

[LINDA *and* JEFF.]

LINDA: Harry. Harry. Here a minute.

JEFF: Don't tell him. It doesn't matter.

LINDA: Here, Harry. Come over here.

HARRY: What's the matter? What's up?

JEFF: It's nothing.

LINDA: Tell him what happened at St Ives, will you?

HARRY: St Ives?

LINDA: Tell him what happened at St Ives.

HARRY: Oh, I see, it's standing in the way of young love's development, is it?

LINDA: Just tell him what happened at St Ives.

HARRY: St Ives. You worried about St Ives, Jeff?

JEFF: Well, I mean, you did go off there; it was the Gretna Green of this generation wasn't it? And now Bagley on his honeymoon.

HARRY: What you worried about it for?

LINDA: Tell him.

HARRY: *You* went camping. Why didn't you go with *him*?

LINDA: He didn't ask.

JEFF: I only had my motor bike and trailer.

HARRY: Only? Only a motor bike and trailer? We had sore feet.

JEFF: Didn't you get lifts then?

HARRY: Lifts? Oh, we twigged on. We twigged on. We let the girls hitch-hike and we hid in the ditch, then, when the cars stopped, there we came, me and Bag, Bag leading the way with billy cans jangling down his arse. Why, the cars took one look, and went.

LINDA: I told you, Jeff. We split up.

HARRY: We split up eventually. Into twos.

JEFF: What? You two, and Bagley and Betty?

LINDA: Listen to him.

HARRY: No, the girls were offered a lift, so we let them take it.

JEFF: When did you get to St Ives?

HARRY: When it was time to turn round and come back. Once you get within twenty miles of St Ives it's like a procession. There's cars bumper to bumper, and beatniks walking along like bloody Indians chewing each other's hair.

JEFF: I thought it was the great time.

HARRY: That's Bagley graphics, mate. Anything else?

JEFF: No, nothing else.

HARRY: Have I done something to heal the breach? Kept the water out?

LINDA: Thanks, Harry.

HARRY: Sure there's nothing else?

JEFF: No. I'm happy. Nothing else.

[HARRY *goes.*]

JEFF: There is something else.

LINDA: What?

JEFF: Did you sleep together in the same tent?

LINDA: Yes. We slept together. Like logs.

JEFF: Like logs?

LINDA: We were worn out.

JEFF: What about Bagley's free love?

LINDA: Bagley's free love? That's good. By the time we got down there we only had three nights at St Ives.

JEFF: Three nights?

LINDA: Three nights. And of those Harry and Douglas were up one night trying to hold the guys in a strong wind; the other night it rained and we'd pitched on low ground. There was one nice night. I remember. That's when Harry had trouble with his anaemicness.

JEFF: Anaemia.

LINDA: Harry suffers from anaemia, he had to go into a boarding house for bed and breakfast and hot blankets.

JEFF: I thought it was a wild orgy.

LINDA: No.

[*Enter* MR BRADBURY.]

FULCHER: Hello, Mr Bradbury.

MR BRADBURY: Hello, Fulcher.

FULCHER: See me arrive then? Come scurrying out?

MR BRADBURY: I saw you arrive. Yes.

FULCHER: Come to chuck me out?

MR BRADBURY: You're very welcome to stay, Fulcher. Very welcome. You're an old boy, very welcome to stay. But the minute you start trouble, you're trespassing.

FULCHER: I won't start trouble, Mr Bradbury.

MR BRADBURY: And don't hang around for Bagley, there's a good lad.

FULCHER: That's O.K., Mr Bradbury. It's just a social call. Social call, come back to see the stay-at-homes.

MR BRADBURY: So long as you and I have an understanding, then there won't be any trouble.

[MR BRADBURY *goes*.]

FULCHER: They're piss scared I'll cause trouble. I went up to see Mr Raines.

GARRET: Did he welcome you?

FULCHER: I saw his secretary. She said 'I'm afraid Mr Raines is busy at the moment, with three businessmen.' I put my foot in the door, there he was, just an excuse . . .

SPOW: Was there nobody there with him?

FULCHER: There were these three fellers, but they were just plants. He said, 'Oh, I'm terribly busy at the moment Fulcher, but you have the freedom of the yard.' I said, 'I'll be around.' That's why he sent Bradbury out – to keep an eye on me.

[*Enter* RAMROD *and* LEO.]

FULCHER: He's sent the bloody spades out now.

GARRET: You can't beat a darkie. It's their heads. Like coconuts.

SPOW: You couldn't hurt that head.

TAFFY: There's only one way to beat a darkie.

HARRY: What's that then?

TAFFY: And there's only one man ever beat them.

ALL: Jimmy Wilde.

TAFFY: And he knew how to beat them.

DICKER: How do you beat them?

TAFFY: It's no use about the head. They're like coconuts. It's the sun. Makes their skulls hard. Bakes them like clay. That's why you never see a punchdrunk coloured fighter.

JIMMY: How do you beat a coloured darkie then?

TAFFY: In the gut, they've got no gut. In the gut. It's soft down there, all coconut water and pineapples. They don't eat meat.

DICKER: Give him a try, Jimmy.

JIMMY: Should I?

DICKER: Yeah, give him a try.

DICKER: Kid him. Kid him along then hit him in the gut. See him go.

JIMMY: Should I?

ALL: Yeah, go on, Jimmy.

JIMMY: Come on then, Leo, give us a round.

LEO: Sure, when you're twenty-one, Jimmy.

JIMMY: Come on, Leo, I'll show you what I've learned.

LEO: Go to hell, will you Jimmy?

JIMMY: Come on, Leo, give us a go. Try this then, Leo.
    [JIMMY *hits* LEO *in the gut. No effect.* LEO *clips him one.*]

LEO: You want to stick to your training schedule, Jimmy, if you want to make good. [*He goes.*]

JIMMY: I thought you said their guts were soft.

SPOW: He must be a well-fed bleeder, that 'un.

JIMMY: I'm not fighting again. And that's for certain. I'm finished. Ramrod, he's had his chance. I'm done.

SPOW: Funny about that. Mebbe he's a throwback. He might have a weak skull.

DICKER: Could you have taken him, Fulch?

FULCHER: I know what you're trying to do. You're trying to put me off Bagley. But I won't be turned aside. I'm after the Bagley, I can tell you. And when he gets back, he's for it.

    [*Enter* MR BRADBURY.]

JIMMY: Here he comes, Snowy. Whiter than white Mr Bradbury.

MR BRADBURY: That's enough from you, Passmore.

JIMMY: And Mr Bradbury bowls from the Gas Tank end, just a trace of hip movement, and he bowls a maiden over. Come on, fellers, join in.

MR BRADBURY: Passmore, stand here, come here, I want you.

JIMMY: Anyone for tennis then, Mr Bradbury, you have a white spot on your grey overall.

MR BRADBURY: Shut up, Passmore. Or I'll have you in front of Mr Raines.

JIMMY: What have I done?

MR BRADBURY: I've heard enough from you, Passmore.

JIMMY: What you calling me Passmore for?

MR BRADBURY: I'm calling you Passmore because I'm sick to death of your attitude.

JIMMY: I haven't been called Passmore since I was at school.

MR BRADBURY: I called you Jimmy often enough. I tried to be friendly with you. I wanted to treat you like a father, but no, you wouldn't have it. You thought you were big, running about with Bagley. I promised your mother I would look after you, but you give me a load of second-hand cheek, so I wash my hands of you, Passmore. I'm sorry, if you don't buck up your ideas, Passmore, I'll tell your mother I can't do anything with you . . .

JIMMY: Don't say that, Mr Bradbury.

MR BRADBURY: The disappointments you've caused me is nobody's business, but I don't have to take it all the time, I can wash my hands of you completely, and you're in for a shock when Bagley gets back because Bagley will be a married man and have other things to do than run around leading you astray. Now *piss off*.

SPOW: It's about time you put your bloody foot down, Mr Bradbury.

MR BRADBURY: Another thing, about this football, if you don't stop that banging about, Mr Raines will stop it by a factory order, make it a ruling. I've fought for years to stop him making a factory order; you lads don't know that, don't know that behind the scenes I'm your representative.

HARRY: I didn't know you were our welfare officer up there, Mr Bradbury.

MR BRADBURY: You know nothing, son. I just kept the football going to give Wags his chance. I can do no more. You don't realize what I go through to preserve your rights. Football. It was me got you permission to paint that goal-post up. And the firm's paint.

[*Enter* WAGS. *Big uproar. He carries his overalls.*]

DICKER: Did you get an offer then, Wags?

VOICES: Come on, Wags. What did Matt say? Was there an offer?

ALL: Wags for United. Wags for United.

WAGS: I played in the trial. There was lads there who'd played for the England Youth. I was great. Played well. The big pitch suited me ...

DICKER: And the turf ...

WAGS: And the turf. I played well, fitted in, like, I was doing things I didn't get a chance to do with the firm's team ...

DICKER: Did you get an offer?

WAGS: Yes. I got an offer. My Dad was locked in with Matt Busby for three hours, but he came out, said I had to finish my apprenticeship first.

VOICE: Finish your apprenticeship?

WAGS: I said to my Dad, 'Dad, you must be joking. There must be ten thousand greasy-arsed fitters in England but there's only one George Best ...' but he said I couldn't go.

BOSWELL: He's crying.

DICKER: Leave him alone. Leave him. Sure, Wags.

MR BRADBURY: All right, just ignore the lad. Let him go.

JEFF: You'll be all right when you're twenty-one, Wags?

WAGS: Don't talk like a bloody big idiot.

JIMMY: You'll still have your skill, Wags.

WAGS: Don't talk like idiots. Twenty-one? Don't talk like idiots.

TAFFY: He's right. Leave him alone. There's no consoling the lad. Only the moon is good enough when you're his age. Disperse and leave him be.

[*Enter* BAGLEY.]

BAGLEY: Aye! aye! aye!... I'm back. What the hell's this? All in mourning because I'm married? *I'm* enjoying it.

DICKER: It's Wags, he got an offer from Matt, but his Dad won't let him take it.

BAGLEY: Why the big, daft, brewery cart driving knacker bag.

MR BRADBURY: Leave him be, Bagley.

BAGLEY: Mr Bradbury, I've been on my honeymoon, but I haven't grown bloody daffodils out of my ears. There, Wags, did Matt make an offer?

WAGS: I was given terms, Bag.

BAGLEY: And that silly bloody Guinness vendor wouldn't take them?

WAGS: He said I had to finish my apprenticeship.

BAGLEY: Does he know there's half a million greasy-arsed fitters in England but only one George Best?

WAGS: I told him that, Bag. I told him that.

SPOW: He'll be all right when he's twenty-one.

BAGLEY: Twenty-one. Twenty-one. Might as well be fifty-one.

MR BRADBURY: He's only trying to help, Bagley.

BAGLEY: You've got to get in at this level. And play yourself in. You can't join them at twenty-one, you'd be an old man.

JEFF: It might be right to finish your apprenticeship. Get a trade behind you. You might go footballing and end up a labourer. Same with boxers, they have a quick career, then finish.

BAGLEY: In this day and age? You talk like an idiot for a clever feller, Jeff. How many footballers are has-beens this day and age? George Best runs a boutique, Danny Blanchflower is on telly, others are writing sports news, the only ones on the scrap heap are those who have no more sense. But Wags is an intelligent boy, it shows in his football. It's a tragedy.

WAGS: What can I do, Doug?

BAGLEY: Come on, have a kick. Give us a kick, Dicker.

SPOW: Are you playing in your honeymoon suit, Bag?

BAGLEY: It had worse treatment at St Ives. Come on, Wags.

WAGS: I'm not touching a ball any more, Bag.

BAGLEY: That's what the reformed prostitute said, Wags, but there's no denying instinct, young 'un.

WAGS: What can I do, Bag? I'm beat. All ends.

BAGLEY: You're not beat, Wags.

WAGS: I've just got to accept it, I'm under age.

BAGLEY: Well don't just *accept* it, beat against it; go back home and kick up merry hell. Give them no rest. Shake the happy household up. Make their life a misery. Have a chip on your shoulder, this is how great link men are made. What if Bobby Charlton had stayed at home? Be brave, Wags.

WAGS: Do you think I should? Kick up a fuss?

BAGLEY: Give them hell, Wags. What do they want you to do? Wait till you're twenty-one?

WAGS: Yes.

BAGLEY: You'll be finished by then. You've got to get used to working with your own class of player before you can start in football. A right clown you'd look on 'Match of the Day' after five years with the works team.

WAGS: That's what I said.

BAGLEY: Protest. Kick up. Howl. Never keep quiet. Kick your front window in, throw your drawing board from the top bedroom, bust your slide-rule, create merry hell. Betty's going to create merry hell when she sees these shoes.

WAGS: I've got to, Bag, I've got to, haven't I?

BAGLEY: I tell you what, Wags, if you don't take your chances while young, you'll regret them for the rest of your life. I'd have been broken-hearted if they hadn't let me marry and be a father.

WAGS: You're right, Bag.

BAGLEY: Bloody am right. And don't you forget it. Hi, Harry. Give us the ball. Come on, get a game organized.

[*They start a game.* FULCHER *appears on the wall.*]

FULCHER: Where's Bagley? I've come to tame him.

SPOW: He's tamed already.

FULCHER: I've come to keep a date with you, Bagley.

BAGLEY: You wouldn't hit a man in his honeymoon suit?

FULCHER: Talk your way out of this one then. Are you ready then, Bag?

BAGLEY: I've just come back from my honeymoon, Fulch. Where's your etiquette?

GARRET: He's bloody weak.

FULCHER: Trying to keep me talking till the buzzer goes, eh? Then you'll dash in and get behind Mr Raines.

BAGLEY: Your karate kick would go through both of us, wouldn't it?

FULCHER: You wouldn't nobbit boy. You wouldn't nobbit.

JIMMY: He talks like a soldier, Bag.

FULCHER: You wouldn't nobbit boy. I am a bloody soldier.

WAGS: Why don't you go in, Doug? It isn't fair. He's trained.

FULCHER: You wouldn't nobbit boy. Wait till you see my knee flicks.

GARRET: You better keep your legs crossed, Bagley.

FULCHER: Right, I'm coming down, Bagley. I've waited for this.

BAGLEY: You looked trained up to the false teeth.

FULCHER: I've been camping out at Aldershot.

WAGS: What you going to do about his unarmed combat, Doug?

BAGLEY: You better pass me that shovel.

FULCHER: Do you remember the last time, Bagley?

BAGLEY: The last time you blew your nose? I don't remember.

FULCHER: Don't rouse me, Bagley, if I lose control these hands can kill.

BAGLEY: In for a pound, feller.

FULCHER: And this wall won't keep me from you, Bagley. This wall is nothing. We jump from higher platforms than this in training. And onto cobbles. You've got to know how to land, use your pivots. It's a matter of landing and rolling. Landing and rolling. Relaxation. That's the key to it . . . tuck and roll . . . tuck and roll . . .

HARRY: Well, Doug, you're in for it now.

FULCHER: I'm coming then, Bagley.

ALL: Ten, nine, eight, seven, six, five, four, three –

[*Enter* MR BRADBURY.]

MR BRADBURY: Fulcher. You're trespassing.

ALL: – two, one, zero.

[FULCHER *jumps. Loud snap.*]

MR BRADBURY: Send for Ramrod, send for the Ambulance, for God's sake. This lad has no right in the paratroopers with these bones.

SPOW: I've seen stronger driftwood.

MR BRADBURY: Give him air, will you? Give him air. He needs air to these bones.

[*Enter* RAMROD.]

MR BRADBURY: I think it's a break, Ramrod, in the femur.

RAMROD: I don't want a load of advice before I start. Give him air. He needs air.

MR BRADBURY: This lad has no right in the paratroopers with these bones.

RAMROD: You don't know it's bones. Let's not have a load of advice before we start. Get that stretcher unrolled, Jimmy. Give him a hand, somebody.

MR BRADBURY: Look, that femur's broke.

BOSWELL: Don't look, Mabel. His foot's pointing the wrong way.

RAMROD: Get him on. A reliable hand at the front of that stretcher, right, lift.

MR BRADBURY: What is it, Ramrod?

RAMROD: Break. Femur. This lad has no right in the paratroopers with these bones.

FULCHER: Bagley, if you've affected my career in the air, I'll kill you.

[*They go off.*]

HARRY: Well, you did it again, Bag.

BAGLEY: Christ, if he did the jumping I've done this fortnight his bones would sound like a bag of dog biscuits.

HARRY: Aren't you worried, Bag?

BAGLEY: Of course I am, I've got to support a wife and family.

[*Hooter goes.*]

Go on, you lot. In with you. Go on, slaves. I'll have a two shilling winner on the two-thirty.

HARRY: What's running?

BAGLEY: Bagley's luck.

HARRY: I said 'what's running' not 'what's running out'.

[*They all go. Enter ALICIA.*]

ALICIA: Douglas, I might have known it was you.

BAGLEY: You got the cards.

ALICIA: Yes.

BAGLEY: Good taste?

ALICIA: Perfect.

BAGLEY: Betty picked them. If I'd had my choice I'd have curled your Dad's hair.

ALICIA: I knew you would.

BAGLEY: We came back early for the trains, they're deadly tomorrow.

ALICIA: I know. Don't excuse yourself.

BAGLEY: I'm not.

ALICIA: Betty told me on the card.

BAGLEY: Oh.

ALICIA: Anyway, it's good to have you back, Douglas. Life hasn't been the same without you.

BAGLEY: Has it not?

ALICIA: No. Honestly. Which way are you going out?

BAGLEY: Over the wall, I thought.

ALICIA: No you're not. Come with me. I'll take your arm.

BAGLEY: This is great. To be just good friends.

ALICIA: I have a motive.

BAGLEY: What?

ALICIA: I want to be the godmother, don't I?

[*They go.*]

SCENE FOUR

The End.

BAGLEY: Come on, lads, give us a kick then. How's that for a bit of the old-fashioned style?

GARRET: Watch what you're doing.

SPOW: Grow up, Bagley.

BAGLEY: And take my place on the side lines? Never.

SPOW: Don't know how you have any energy left, Bagley.

BAGLEY: Thank God the football season's on us Dicker.

DICKER: It won't be the same without Wags.

BAGLEY: He's got his first match for the United reserves next Saturday.

JIMMY: They say Mr Raines went to see his Dad to let him go.

BAGLEY: Mr Raines like hell. It was me got him away. Applied psychology. I went up to him, 'If you don't let Wags go,' I said, 'I'll punch a hole through the back of your head.'

BOSWELL: I heard it was the doctor.

DICKER: It wasn't the doctor.

BOSWELL: I heard the doctor said if Wags didn't go he'd be ill. Mentally ill.

BAGLEY: You've heard the wrong story.

DICKER: It was my Dad. My Dad did it. He said to Wags' Dad, 'Ever since the breathalyser you've gone illogical. You ought to get off the brewery wagons, get a driving job where you can get drunk on the job.'

BAGLEY: What's he driving? The Electricity Board lift?

DICKER: He's driving a tipper. He's drunk all the time. He's his old self. That's why he let Wags go.

[*Enter* FULCHER.]

FULCHER: Hi, lads. He's having me back.

ALL: Hooh. Never. Bloody hell. Can we not get rid of you?

FULCHER: He's having me back. When I get my papers. Semi-skilled, but I'll have my own machine. I won't be on the floor. Not sweeping. He's getting Pakistanis in. [*He sits down with* SPOW *and* GARRET.] Good of him, eh? Semi-skilled. I'm glad about that. And I'll have a pension.

SPOW: Pension? At eighteen? You won't have a pension.

FULCHER: My solicitor said I'll have a pension.

GARRET: You got a solicitor?

FULCHER: 'Course I got a solicitor. I need one with my bones. And I got a specialist. Hi. Not a bad day. Look at that sky. Good sky for jumping.

GARRET: Bit windy.

FULCHER: Windy skies don't trouble you. It's the hot buggers that get you. Thermals.

SPOW: Hot air?

FULCHER: Yeah. Our battalion went to the Big Desert in Arabia. What the hell do they call it?

SPOW: Sahara?

FULCHER: Get stuffed.

GARRET: I know the one.

FULCHER: I'll tell you where it is. It's where Lawrence of Arabia fought. The Big Desert it's called. It's got an Arabic name, like, but the English name is ... what is it? I think it's the Big Desert.

GARRET: What were you doing out there?

FULCHER: I wasn't there. I nearly went. Our mob went. But I had my accident.

GARRET: What was your mob doing out there?

FULCHER: Twisting about in these thermals.

SPOW: Were they asked to go out?

FULCHER: Yeah, there was this Sheik like, this is how the story started, there was this Sheik, and he was loaded. Oil.

SPOW: Them Sheiks is loaded, with oil.

GARRET: All the big firms keep them in power, Shell, B.P., all that.

SPOW: Esso.

GARRET: I'm not sure about Esso.

SPOW: Bloody Esso, I'm telling you.

FULCHER: Anyhow, this loaded Sheik was a right bastard to his people. He suppressed them, he wouldn't let them have no democracy, he wouldn't let them have transistor radios or air conditioning or anything of that. And it's bloody hot out there. He had two sons, and the eldest one like, got this idea to come over to England, and get educated. Oxford.

SPOW: That's the wogs all over, isn't it?

GARRET: Oh, you can't stop them. In the war, at the Sweet Water Canal, we used to treat them like crap, put the boot in, stand on their bare feet, and they'd do anything for the gelt. Then after the bloody war, come over here to get educated. And us silly sods get back to work.

FULCHER: Anyhow, this one came to Oxford, got ideas, he saw what it was like here, pictures, cars, got himself a white tart. Went back to the Sheik, his father ... and said, 'What about letting our people have freedom and democracy, transistor radios and that?' Know what his father did?

SPOW: What?

FULCHER: Shot the sod.

SPOW: All that bloody money, eh, and no morality.

FULCHER: Shot him. So the younger son thought, 'I better piss off out of this,' so he got himself some men, and arms, trucks and that off the Russians, and went into this bloody big desert. I wish I could remember its name. It was in the picture.

GARRET: What picture?

FULCHER: *Lawrence of Arabia*. Hi, Taffy Doorman, what do they call that desert where Lawrence of Arabia was?

TAFFY: The Empty Quarter.

FULCHER: That's it. That's it. The Empty Quarter. Did you see the picture?

TAFFY: No, I read *Seven Pillars of Wisdom*.

FULCHER: I wonder what that had to do with it? Anyway,

the Sheik applied to the British Government to send out troops to crush the son . . . and our lads went out.

GARRET: What happened?

FULCHER: They crushed the sod.

SPOW: That'll learn him.

GARRET: Keeps the oil flowing. You've got to butter up them Sheiks.

[*Enter* BETTY.]

GARRET: There's Bagley's missus. Look at the size of her.

SPOW: She shouldn't be standing at a machine like that. It'll play havoc with her legs.

FULCHER: Will it?

SPOW: It'll play hell with her legs. She'll lose them good legs.

TAFFY: Hello, Mrs Bagley.

BAGLEY: Are you being funny, Taffy Doorman?

TAFFY: Of course I'm not being funny. The woman is entitled to her title, isn't she?

BAGLEY: She is, isn't she. Say 'hello' to the man, Betty.

BETTY: I've said 'hello'.

BAGLEY: Good old Taffy. Nobody else calls her Mrs Bagley yet. Except the milkman, and that's a bad sign.

BETTY: Here a minute, Douglas.

BAGLEY: Just a minute, love. I'm loosening up. I'm just finding peak form.

BETTY: Here a minute, I want you.

BAGLEY: I'm here. Now what?

BETTY: Linda said we could apply for social.

BAGLEY: Did she now?

BETTY: Yes.

LINDA: I think you can, Douglas.

BAGLEY: But we're not hard up.

LINDA: It's your rights, if you've paid your dues.

BETTY: Alicia is on the phone now.

BAGLEY: Oh, Alicia will fix it.

BETTY: She's being a good friend, Douglas. She's very helpful.

BAGLEY: I know, but she's a fixer. If we're not careful

we'll be collecting our maternity grant from the Tennis Club.

BETTY: Anyway, she's on the phone, and she thinks ... are you listening?

BAGLEY: Give us a kick Dicker.

BETTY: Are you listening? She thinks that because we were married on the eighth, and you're not twenty-one till August, then, if the baby is due in March ...

BAGLEY: It'll be twin girls. Alicia ought to go in for astrology.

LINDA: You ought to listen, Douglas.

BAGLEY: Look, you fix it. I'll listen, I'm getting on with the game.

BETTY: The game can wait.

BAGLEY: That's not what Francis Drake said. [*He goes.*]
 [*Enter* RAMROD.]

RAMROD: Jimmy, Leo, come on, get in. Serious training.

DICKER: Jimmy, I thought you were packing it in, taking up karate.

JIMMY: Ramrod has offered me a place in the tournament.

FULCHER: You can't do karate, Jimmy.

JIMMY: No, but I can walk without a stick.

RAMROD: Come on now, lads. Leo, are you ready?

LEO: Sure, Ramrod.

BAGLEY: Hi, Leo, you're getting to be a champ, aren't you? I tell you what, you can marry my daughter. How's that for race relations? Up you, Powell.

TAFFY: You're not letting Jimmy enter the tournament, are you, Ramrod? Have you no mercy?

RAMROD: That lad needs a tournament. Don't worry, don't worry. I'll phone around my mates in the game, get an opponent like him, we'll make them wear cushions, head guards, jock straps; if they walked under a bus they wouldn't get hurt. And I'll be in the corner throwing in the towel the minute one of them looks like landing a punch. This is a prime example of what sport can do for character. [*He goes.*]

[ALICIA *and* LINDA *and* BETTY.]

BETTY: Douglas, here. Douglas, come on.

BETTY: Alicia has been on the phone. Now listen.

BAGLEY: I'm all ears.

ALICIA: I've been on the phone. Now you've got your milk tokens, Betty?

BETTY: Yes.

ALICIA: And you've got your orange tokens?

BETTY: Yes.

ALICIA: You're all stamped up and you've been to the pre-natal. Now this is the situation as I got it on the phone from the Social Security. You are entitled to a maternity grant of twenty-two pounds. For baby things, like cot and so forth; but, eleven weeks before the baby is due, you can also claim benefit of four pounds a week. Now, if Betty can work till then ...

BETTY: I think I can manage.

ALICIA: Well, if you can, the firm will pay your wage, and your stamp. Now, it is up to you whether you keep your stamp up once you're having the baby, because if you *come* back to work ...

BAGLEY: But she's going to be a mother.

ALICIA: But if she comes back to work, you must go to the Ministry of Pensions and National Insurance, see about putting your *own* stamp on, and claim your maternity benefit, and as Douglas isn't yet twenty-one, and you were married on the eighth ...

BAGLEY: Here we go, Rodney will be in with the forceps in a minute.

LINDA: Be sensible, Douglas. Not that it's any of my business.

BAGLEY: The way your ears are flapping I'd have thought you and Jeff had been up to something.

ALICIA: Now listen. As Douglas isn't out of his time yet, he can see the firm's Welfare Officer, to get in touch with the Social Security people, and they can send a social worker round to see how you're living, and you might be able to claim National Assistance.

BAGLEY: I'm not claiming National Assistance. My mother wouldn't let me.

ALICIA: But you are unable to support a wife.

BAGLEY: Who said that?

ALICIA: We can make out a case.

BAGLEY: Well don't bloody bother. I've got a family. My Mam's giving us the back room for nothing, and our Dad will come forth with a bit of beer money. Don't give me social security, and visitors, I'm not spastic. Give us a kick then, Dicker.

BETTY: Douglas. Come back here this minute.

BAGLEY: Give us a kick.

BETTY: Come back here this minute, Douglas Bagley.

BAGLEY: You work it out, and I'll sign it. Give it an X Certificate.

[*Enter* JEFF *from drawing office.*]

DICKER: Hya, Jeff?

BOSWELL: Hya, Jeff. Jeff, can you spare a minute? It's my homework, Jeff. The second year on maths. It's these. I can't understand them. Give me a minute, Jeff.

[*They go into a confab.*]

DICKER: What's it like up there then, Jeff?

JEFF: Great, Dick. What you want to realize, Bos, is that the formula applies to the algebraic system . . . now look . . . Jimmy understood this, so you should.

VOICE: Do you get tea brought by long-legged typists, Jeff?

JEFF: Hah, sure do . . . did you get that? If x is the constant and y is the variable, then you're only left to find the standard voltage.

BOSWELL: Think I'll ever do it, Jeff?

JEFF: Sure you will, and don't be frightened to ask. You and Jimmy ought to work together. It's easier when there are two of you.

VOICE: They've got a little water machine you can drink out of, haven't they, Jeff?

JEFF: Sure.

VOICE: What's it like starting at nine in the morning?

JEFF: I miss seeing the stars.

VOICE: Are you on day release for classes, Jeff?

JEFF: Yes, I go three days a week up the Tech.

VOICE: You ought to take a degree. Like Leo.

SPOW: Did you hear that?

GARRET: Jeff is ten times better than Leo.

JEFF: I'm sorry, Garretty. I hate to refute your theories, but he's more qualified than I am.

GARRET: You'll catch him up, Jeff. You stick in. You'll catch him up.

JEFF: For the honour of the race.

BAGLEY: What do they let you do up there then, Jeff? Sharpen pencils on the Emery cloth?

JEFF: I'm in on this Modernizing Section, Bag. The section leader has put me on it. In a very humble capacity, I'm just copying drawings, but I'm in that section.

BAGLEY: I could modernize it for them, just give me a tub of high explosives.

JEFF: You won't recognize the place when the new power plant is built. You'll be able to work with a collar and tie on. And white overalls. [He goes.]

TAFFY: Good luck to him. If he wants to work to get on. The choice is yours. In this trade you can end up your life a greasy-arsed fitter or you can be in charge of the engines in the Queen Elizabeth.

GARRET: Who wants to join the Queen Elizabeth? Anyway, I get my kicks on a fishing boat at Brid.

BAGLEY [peering over BOSWELL's shoulder]: That old stuff. Nursery rhymes in algebraic form.

BOSWELL: It comes in a flash, you know, Bag. You're in the dark, and then it comes in a flash.

BAGLEY: Don't I know it.

BOSWELL: Algebra.

BAGLEY: How are you and Mabel making out?

BOSWELL: We're saving for a deposit on a flat.

BAGLEY: Flat! But you haven't even kissed her yet.

BOSWELL: Whatever we haven't done, it's no use getting married without a roof over your head.

BAGLEY: That's an old wives' tale. I've managed. Just get married and let love find its own way.

BOSWELL: I'm having a deposit.

BAGLEY: Get your name down for a council house.

BOSWELL: We've gone into it. Listen, if you put down two hundred pounds, on a flat for eight hundred, at five and a half, and say the rateable value is thirty-six pound, and you take up the option . . .

BAGLEY: *Don't* you start. There's Mabel, go and give her a kiss, if it's in the Almanac for this month.

[*Enter* HARRY *in suit.*]

BAGLEY: Hi, Harry, why the suit?

HARRY: I've been in town.

BAGLEY: Give out, give out. What's got over you? Trying to get in the drawing office?

HARRY: No. I'm trying to get away, Bag.

BAGLEY: We're all trying that, aren't we?

HARRY: I've been for an interview.

BAGLEY: Interview? Getting out of the trade?

HARRY: Merchant Navy.

BAGLEY: They won't take you in the Merchant Navy.

HARRY: They will. I've got it. I'm going.

BAGLEY: I like that. You're leaving me? Without a word? Without a single sentence, you're off?

HARRY: I'll be off in a month.

BAGLEY: In a month? I thought it took years.

HARRY: I'm off training. In a month.

BAGLEY: Where do you train?

HARRY: Essex.

BAGLEY: Harry. You can't do this to me. Will you be an officer?

HARRY: Yes. When I've trained.

BAGLEY: But you haven't got a trade.

HARRY: They're teaching me the trade. I'm going with Marconi.

BAGLEY: Who the hell's Marconi? I thought he sold ice lollies.

HARRY: It's the radio firm. Marconi's.

BAGLEY: You going in for radio then?

HARRY: Yeah. Ops.

BAGLEY: Ops? That sounds good.

HARRY: I've wanted to get away for a long time. But I didn't want to be an engineer. I thought of being a Steward, but my Dad said he'd heard rumours about Stewards, so I got in on radio instead. Then I'll get on a line.

BAGLEY: Hell. That sounds romantic. What about your anaemia?

HARRY: I'll go on tropical routes. I passed my medical O.K.

BAGLEY: Yeah, well good luck, Harry. Remember the *Titanic*. [*He goes.*]

JEFF: Hi, Harry, how did you do?

BAGLEY: Was he in on the secret then?

HARRY: I had to tell Jeff.

BAGLEY: You didn't tell Bagley.

HARRY: I didn't want it all over the yard, Doug.

[BAGLEY *to* SPOW. GARRET *and* FULCHER.]

BAGLEY: Hi, Garretty, you say you go fishing week-ends?

GARRET: Yeah. Me and Spow. Brid.

BAGLEY: Didn't think you had it in you.

GARRET: There's more cod been in me than there has in the North Sea.

SPOW: Cod's good for you, Bagley, if your powers are weakening.

BAGLEY: When do you get away?

SPOW: Friday night.

BAGLEY: Come back Saturday?

SPOW: Do we hell, Sunday night.

GARRET: It means missing church. Want to come?

BAGLEY: Thinking about it.

GARRET: We go in a party. There's two fellers from the Pattern Shop come, one from the Foundry, and us. You could join.

BAGLEY: How much does it flay you for?

GARRET: Petrol, among five, in a van ten bob apiece. Hire

of boat, quid apiece, bed and breakfast, quid apiece, unless we sleep in the van; beer, well . . . brings it up to a fiver. You'd get away with a fiver.

BAGLEY: It's a lot of money.

GARRET: Getting cautious in your old age, Bag?

BAGLEY: No. Costs me that to get my haircut.

SPOW: It gets you away from the house.

GARRET: Out of sight of the missus.

SPOW: You've got to plan your life, Bag.

GARRET: No use staying at home all the time.

BAGLEY: A fiver?

GARRET: Count you in?

BAGLEY: I'll work it out.

SPOW: You bring plenty of fish home on Sunday night, keeps the missus quiet.

GARRET: You've got to dictate your terms *now*, Bag. If you're asking for a night out now, you'll never get any better. You've got to *tell her* what you're having straight away, now, and stick to it. Otherwise, if she starts dictating the terms . . . you've had it.

BAGLEY: But I love the lass.

GARRET: We all love it, but the less you see of it the better you like it.

SPOW: I had a week-end with the wife and family last summer, when we didn't go away. Murder it was. Agony. By the end, she said, 'For Christ's sake, go fishing next week.'

GARRET: That's how you want it. So they're glad to let you go.

BAGLEY: Sure. Well I'll let you know.

SPOW: We'll squeeze you in the van. Do it now and it won't be painful to her. Delay and you miss your chance.

BAGLEY: Delay and you miss your chance.

[*To* FULCHER.] Hi there, Fulch, all right?

FULCHER: Aye.

BAGLEY: Well *I'm* bloody fed up. I was just stood down there and Harry walks right in out of the blue and tells me he's going in the Merchant Navy. Me best mate! I don't know. Everybody's leaving now or getting married; just 'cause I started it. Jeff and Linda, they'll be next. Then Mabel and Boswell, then Alicia entering the birth pill zone. . . . I'm bloody fed up. Look at them two, Spow and Garret seem to be getting no older, I feel as though I'm catching them up, reserve me a place there, fellers, I'll bring my thermos. Some hopes of that.

[ALICIA *to* BAGLEY.]

ALICIA: Douglas. Betty's gone in to give her legs a rest. Just to get them up off the floor.

BAGLEY: Oh, thanks Alice.

ALICIA: I'm not happy about them, Douglas.

BAGLEY: What?

ALICIA: Betty's legs.

BAGLEY: She's got lovely legs. They'll trim down after the baby.

ALICIA: No, I'm thinking of the varicose. I'd have the doctor to have another look at them. He didn't like them last time.

BAGLEY: Did he not?

ALICIA: Didn't she tell you?

BAGLEY: Must have done. It's all we talk about at nights. Trips to the doctor's.

ALICIA: Well. You know. It would be terrible if she had trouble. Just for the extra money.

BAGLEY: She can knock off work now for all I care, Alice.

ALICIA: Did Betty tell you I'm phoning Gregory this afternoon? Do you mind?

BAGLEY: Who the hell's Gregory, and why shouldn't he be phoned?

ALICIA: Gregory is in the estate business.

BAGLEY: What estate's that?

ALICIA: Housing.

BAGLEY: Council housing?

ALICIA: No. Private. Anyway, I thought a ring might not do any harm, to look into the flat situation.

BAGLEY: We're quite all right where we are. With Mam.

ALICIA: I know, Betty loves it with your Mam, but we thought it would do no harm to inquire . . .

BAGLEY: Oh.

ALICIA: For when the baby comes.

BAGLEY: My Mam will love the baby.

ALICIA: Shall I not inquire then?

BAGLEY: Well, if Betty said.

ALICIA: I think she fancies the idea, and you know what women are, putting up their own curtains and that.

BAGLEY: Yeah. Thanks, Alice. What's in it for you?

ALICIA: I want to be godmother, don't I?

[*Enter* MR BRADBURY. *He goes across to the notice-board.*]

VOICE: Orders for the day, is it, Mr Bradbury? Safety shoes must be worn by order of Mr Raines.

VOICE: What is it then, Mr Bradbury? It looks a fuss.

MR BRADBURY: If you'd bother to look you might find a surprise.

BAGLEY: Come on, lads, make a game.

MR BRADBURY: What you standing there for? It won't come to you. And none of you can see from that distance.

FULCHER: I had to read smaller print than that from ten feet at my medical.

VOICE: What is it?

DICKER: It's lists of awards, apprentice awards.

[*They all rush to see.*]

VOICES: Am I on? Let me see, don't push. That's my name. Best Lathe turning . . . Proficiency in Brass Test Piece . . . Apprentice Craftsmanship . . .

BAGLEY: Look at them all. Have they all got cup fever then? Do you all want bloody Oscars?

MR BRADBURY: It's no use pretending you don't care, Bagley.

BAGLEY: Believe it or not, I don't care.

MR BRADBURY: You'll have to start caring, some day.

BAGLEY: Not this kid, I've had better free gifts with a packet of corn flakes.

MR BRADBURY: You a married man and still no sense of responsibility.

BAGLEY: You sound like the insurance man.

MR BRADBURY: No use sending the insurance man to you, you don't plan a week ahead.

BAGLEY: I don't need insurance, I'm a welder, my muscles are my insurance.

MR BRADBURY: Still no sense.

BAGLEY: You've got no bloody sense, of humour. Come on, now let's get on with a game.

VOICES: Hang on. Who got the Set Piece award ... where's the Drilling and Boring? ... Successful Studies and General Merit ... Dicker ... Award for Shopwork and Time keeping ... that's not Bagley.

[*Enter a* NEW APPRENTICE.]

BAGLEY: New apprentice, lads. When we get a new apprentice.

APPRENTICE: Piss off, you.

BAGLEY: The little sod kicked. Get him, lads.

[APPRENTICE *scampers off. A few of them catch him.*]

BAGLEY: When we get a new ... hold him ... get the grease.

JEFF: Stop. Bagley. Doug, leave him, leave him.

BAGLEY: Go back to your drawing office, mate.

JEFF: Grow up will you, Doug? If you could see yourself from where I'm standing. You're a married man.

BAGLEY: Come on, lads, when we get a new apprentice.

JEFF: Doug. Leave off Doug. You look pathetic.

BAGLEY: You shouldn't have said that, Jeff.

JEFF: I'm telling you, you look pathetic. A married man greasing a kid.

BAGLEY: I said you shouldn't have said that. What are you going to do about it?

JEFF: I'm going to do nothing about it. Not by your style.

BAGLEY: Do you think I might break your drawing finger, is that it? I might injure the golden hands.

JEFF: Don't push, Doug. You're just making it worse for yourself.

BAGLEY: Worse for *my* self?

JEFF: Yes. They've grown out of it. So should you.

BAGLEY: [*Looking around at the lack of support*]: O.K., Jeff. Leave him be. Shake on it, Jeff. No hard feelings. Come on, give me your hand.

JEFF: None of Fulcher's wrist flicks or shoulder tosses?

BAGLEY: I don't know how to do them. I'm a nose-punching man myself. Shake on it, Jeff. How's the kid? He looks a proper bantie cock. Fit and chirpy.

APPRENTICE: You only caught me because I twisted my ankle.

BAGLEY: Never mind, kid, you'll live.

SPOW: The old traditions are going fast, aren't they, Bag?

BAGLEY: Yeah.

FULCHER: You should have seen the initiation in the army. They reckon the paras have the hardest initiation in the world.

GARRET: Come on, Bag. Sit down, have a cup. There, pour him a cup.

BAGLEY: When did you say you were going fishing?

SPOW: This week-end, Friday night.

GARRET: You coming?

BAGLEY: What if the weather's too rough when you get there?

SPOW: We never forecast. Getting cautious, Bag?

GARRET: Need a barometer?

BAGLEY: No.

SPOW: Are you coming then?

BAGLEY: I'll sort it out with the wife.

GARRET: That's it. Your sorting out has got to be done early.

FULCHER: I might go myself. If the boat's steady.

SPOW: There's room for both of you.

FULCHER: How about it, Bags?

BAGLEY: I tell you. I'll sort things out with the wife. I've got a bit of sorting out to do.

SPOW: Mind you. You've got to be sensible, Bags.

BAGLEY: Sensible?

SPOW: You can't go to Brid on National Assistance. You might have to wait a bit.

GARRET: Till you're twenty-one.

[*Hooter goes. They all go in.* APPRENTICE *hangs about.*]

BAGLEY: Go on. I'm last in.

APPRENTICE: Tod you, buck. I'm last in.

BAGLEY: I'm last in, young 'un.

APPRENTICE: You're not. I'm last in.

BAGLEY: Go on, you little sod.

[*They chase around.* APPRENTICE *evades Bagley.*]

TAFFY: Come on, Bagley, get clocked in.

BAGLEY: You last in then, young 'un. I tell you what, you'll have a bloody hard job to keep it!

MORE ABOUT PENGUINS

Penguinews, which appears every month, contains details of all the new books issued by Penguins as they are published. From time to time it is supplemented by *Penguins in Print*, which is a complete list of all books published by Penguins which are in print. (There are well over three thousand of these.)

A specimen copy of *Penguinews* will be sent to you free on request, and you can become a subscriber for the price of the postage – 4s. for a year's issues (including the complete lists). Just write to Dept EP, Penguin Books Ltd, Harmondsworth, Middlesex, enclosing a cheque or postal order, and your name will be added to the mailing list.

Some other books published by Penguins are described on the following pages.

Note: *Penguinews* and *Penguins in Print* are not available in the U.S.A. or Canada

STAIRCASE

NOW A TWENTIETH CENTURY-FOX FILM STARRING REX HARRISON AND RICHARD BURTON

Charles Dyer

Charles Dyer's *Staircase* was the first play to be published in the Penguin Modern Playwrights series and the Royal Shakespeare Company's production, coinciding with publication, established Dyer as a master of the duologue.

Like *Rattle of a Simple Man,* his earlier success, *Staircase* shows Dyer's deep humanity, his wit and passion, his genius in creating great roles for international actors.

FANGHORN

David Pinner

Fanghorn introduces a highly idiosyncratic young English playwright. David Pinner, born in 1940, was awarded an Arts Council Drama Bursary in 1965. His ambition as a dramatist is to reintroduce poetry and all that implies into the theatre. He is concerned with the potential rather than the limitations of humanity. Fanghorn is a purple comedy which shows the necessity of trusting and believing other people, even if other people are untrustworthy and unbelievable.

LEE HARVEY OSWALD

Michael Hastings

Michael Hastings in his new play *Lee Harvey Oswald: a far mean streak of indepence brought on by negleck* is in search of Oswald, the alleged assassin of John F. Kennedy. The action takes place in the courtroom, and in the homes of Oswald, his wife Marina and of his mother. There is no attempt to speculate, but the case is brilliantly followed through its principal areas of doubt.

A PELICAN BOOK

ADOLESCENT BOYS OF EAST LONDON

Peter Willmott

A classic study of boys growing up in Bethnal Green, by one of the authors of *Family and Kinship in East London*.

'Vividly written, this study draws on interviews as well as diaries kept by young men, though all of these are subjected to statistical controls. Essentially Willmott is describing young people *in process*: we see the homes they come from, and the schools they pass through, en route to the world of work and the new families they themselves will create ... suggests some things that might be done to ease the strains of adolescence' – Peter Worsley in the *Guardian*.

'Reads so well, while yet offering facts and ideas of real value to teachers, youth leaders and social workers, that one feels it is almost unfair to the more pedestrian, journalistic offerings of other sociologists. Here one can learn more about teenage boys' attitudes to work, school, youth clubs, delinquency and many other matters of concern, and *enjoy* the learning, too' – *The Times Educational Supplement*.

'It is a model of its kind, exactly on target, impeccably collated and always very readable' – Dennis Potter in *New Society*.

THE NIGEL BARTON PLAYS

Dennis Potter

Dennis Potter's award-winning television comedies are almost savage in the irony they extract from British politics. *Stand Up, Nigel Barton,* the first play, shows his central character contemplating politics as a career – having been a misfit at home, at school and at Oxford. In the second play, *Vote Vote Vote for Nigel Barton,* against a background of intrigue he is a candidate in a rural election, fighting a losing battle in a 'safe' opposition seat. The plays read brilliantly and Dennis Potter has provided a hard-hitting introduction in which he assesses the situation of those writing seriously for television today.

Also by Peter Terson

ZIGGER ZAGGER
MOONEY AND HIS CARAVANS

When the National Youth Theatre performed Peter Terson's *Zigger Zagger*, its hectic pace and shattering impact drove the audience into the obsessed lives of the football fans on the terraces. In the *Sunday Times* J. W. Lambert wrote: 'Peter Terson's astonishing entertainment gains body from its continual tension between surface exhilaration and underlying hopelessness ... Very funny and distinctly alarming, *Zigger Zagger* is true theatre'.

By contrast, *Mooney and His Caravans* is a social drama with a small cast. By turns funny and disturbing, it records the successive stages in the humiliation of a weak husband, and the paradoxical strengthening of the love which his unfaithful wife feels for him.